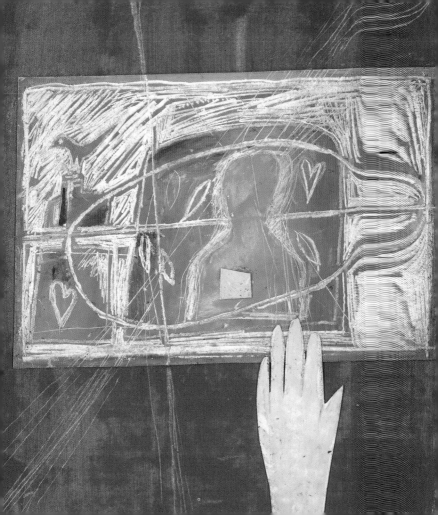

Secrets of

REIKI

ANNE CHARLISH AND
ANGELA ROBERTSHAW

A Dorling Kindersley Book

Dorling DK Kindersley

LONDON, NEW YORK, MUNICH,
MELBOURNE, and DELHI

This book was conceived, designed and produced by
THE IVY PRESS LIMITED,
The Old Candlemakers, Lewes, East Sussex BN7 2NZ

Art director Peter Bridgewater
Editorial director Sophie Collins
Designers Siân Keogh, Sandra Marques
Editor Kim Davies
Picture researcher Mary Devine
Photography David Jordan
Photography organization Kim Davies, Siân Keogh
Illustrations Axis Design Editions Limited, Kuo Kang Chen, Michael Courtney,
Lesley-Anne Hutchings, Andrew Kulman, Stephen Raw, Sarah Young

First published in Great Britain in 2001 by
DORLING KINDERSLEY LIMITED,
80 The Strand, London, WC2R ORL

A Penguin Company

A CIP catalogue record for this book is
available from the British Library

ISBN 0 7513 3562 2

Originated and printed by
Hong Kong Graphics and Printing Limited, China

see our complete
catalogue at

www.dk.com

CONTENTS

Healing from the hands
Secrets of Reiki shows you how
you can use your hands as a
tool for transmitting energy.

HOW TO USE THIS BOOK *Secrets of*
Reiki is a complete guide to this hands-on form of healing. It is suitable for total
beginners and for more experienced students who wish to extend their
knowledge. To make it easy to use, the book has been divided into seven
sections, including chapters on how reiki works and how to make the most of
a treatment. *Secrets of Reiki* guides you through learning the techniques and
giving treatments, step by step. There are also sections on integrating reiki into
daily life and progressing further. A final chapter explains the scope of reiki
and suggests how to use it to its fullest extent.

Important Notice

All the claims and beliefs in this
book have been sincerely made
by reiki masters and practitioners
or their students and clients.
Neither publisher nor author can
be held responsible for any event,
claim, or belief described in this
book. If you have a medical or
psychiatric condition, you are
advised to consult your doctor
before embarking on any course
of reiki. Reiki is not intended to be
a substitute for any medical,
hospital, or psychiatric treatment.

The basics
The first chapters of the book explain
what reiki is and how to learn it.

THE 27 REIKI HAND POSITIONS

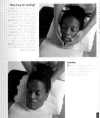

Home practice
*Practical pages like
these show all the
positions for healing.*

The Significance of Hand Positions 1 to 4

Detail
*Black-and-white pages
supplement the practical
pages, giving you the
theory behind each of the
healing positions.*

GIVING SEATED REIKI

Real-life situations
*These pages show you
how to adapt and use
what you have learned.*

Introduction

Rei-Ki
The Japanese letters above show Rei, meaning "universal", and Ki, meaning "life force".

Reiki is a method of using universal energy to enhance well-being. This book focuses on traditional Usui Reiki, also known as Usui Shiki Ryoho. This is a simple, direct, and accessible form of healing. Through a gentle, hands-on technique, reiki is used to bring peace and balance to the mind, body, and spirit. Reiki healing is based on accessing the universal life energy, which is believed by reiki adherents to be part of everyone and everything. Reiki healing is said to be available to everyone, if they choose it to come into their lives.

Meeting reiki

People are often said to be drawn to reiki, even when they know very little about it. Traditionally, the reiki techniques were passed by word of mouth, from master to student. However, in recent years, reiki has become more widespread, and increasing numbers of people are hearing of it through friends, acquaintances, or the media.

Making a commitment

To learn reiki, you need a sincere commitment to helping yourself and others. The techniques for reiki are easily learned and accessible to everyone. However, anyone using the techniques will first need to be attuned, or initiated, by a reiki master.

When first learned, the reiki techniques are primarily used for self-healing or for helping friends and family. Many people use them to help facilitate change or to open up a new way of living. Reiki is said to work on a level of trust. You can have no specific expectations of the healing, for healing is not necessarily curing. Rather, it is about restoring a sense of wholeness and harmony. Many reiki adherents say that reiki has its own wisdom and that it can be empowering even when physical healing is not possible.

Honouring reiki

Respecting the power of reiki and honouring the continuity of its simple traditions can help us to appreciate its value in today's complex world. Learning about the traditions can increase understanding, but true understanding comes only through experience. This book has been produced to help those who wish to discover the experience of reiki for themselves.

Connect to Life

Opening up to reiki gives us a deeper connection to life itself, helping us to discover who we are and our place in the world.

THE HEALING SPIRIT OF REIKI

Everyone has the ability to heal themselves and to help others in their healing process. Universal energy flows through all of us. However, this flow of energy can become blocked during periods of stress and illness. Reiki is an immensely simple yet powerful method of healing, using the hands, which can remove these blockages and restore the flow of energy around the body. The spirit of reiki is challenging and rewarding and can lead you into a journey of spiritual exploration and discovery. This energizing force can empower you to feel as an emotional being, to respond to situations creatively, and to act throughout your life as a channel for good.

What is Reiki?

Drawing energy
The reiki practitioner draws in the life-force energy that is all around us and becomes a conduit for healing.

Reiki is a hands-on healing technique, which is based on the idea of a universal life force. Reiki practitioners believe that it is possible to access this force and use it for healing mind, body, and spirit.

Universal energy

The concept of a life force has been recognized in many cultures for thousands of years, and similar concepts are used in many other complementary therapies, such as acupuncture and shiatsu, as well as in physical and spiritual practices, such as tai chi and yoga. In China this life force is known as *chi*, in Hinduism as *prana*, and by the ancient Egyptians as *ka*.

The beliefs and practice of reiki emerged in nineteenth-century Japan and from there were taken to Hawaii, California, and the Western world. The word reiki itself is made up of "rei", meaning "universal" in Japanese, and "ki", which means "life force".

A natural flow

Reiki practitioners aim to draw energy from the universal life force that is all around us and then let it flow through their hands and into the person who needs the healing.

By laying their hands on various parts of the body in turn, they transmit energy to help restore its natural flow around the recipient's body. This also releases any blockages that may prevent the recipients from reaching their full potential. The effect of reiki is not always immediate or obvious, although for some people it can be dramatic and instant. Reiki is thought by its practitioners to have its own inherent wisdom and act as a force that gives people what they need, rather than what they ask for.

You can receive reiki treatments without having to learn the techniques, but many people progress to learning the techniques from a master.

A spiritual gift

Reiki is often seen as more than a complementary therapy. It can also be regarded as a spiritual journey or a life path. Many people say that the healing and balancing of the body's natural flow of energy create a sense of openness. This offers the opportunity to expand one's consciousness, as well as to release long-held stresses and pains.

The Force of Life

Life force flows through all of us. Reiki healing is simply a means of accessing this energy in a direct and amplified way.

Nourishment and energy
*Just as a flower thrives only
when its basic needs are met,
we all need nurturing to survive.*

AN ENERGIZING FORCE
Reiki is believed by its adherents to be an energizing force that revitalizes and liberates the potential that is within all of us. Energetic force is present in every living thing on earth. Other forms of energy, such as heat and sound waves, pulsate around us all the time although they cannot be seen. All can be viewed as part of the universal life force that is harnessed by reiki practitioners and used as a healing energy to help balance and centre the mind, body, and spirit.

A universal need
*The simplest life forms, such as
young ferns, need energy to
grow and to survive.*

Energy and matter

Through the science of physics, we know that energy holds matter together. The whole universe is a careful balance between energy and matter, from the smallest atom to the greatest star.

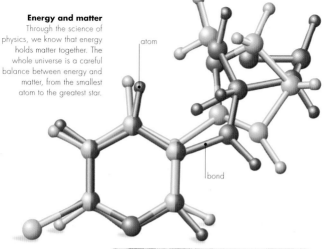

atom

bond

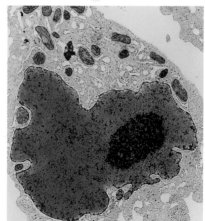

Reiki knows no limits

Reiki energy reaches to the very cells of our bodies, as well as to the cells of other living things.

A Unique System

Revealing aura
The aura surrounding our body changes constantly depending on the state of our well-being.

Reiki is a method of healing that differs from all others. Unlike many systems, it is not directed towards achieving specific ends: the healing is believed to direct itself naturally to wherever it is most needed. The giver acts simply as a channel or conduit, through which the universal energy is drawn into the receiver. Reiki benefits the healer as well as the person receiving the treatment. The life force flows through the healer's energetic system first, transmuting any restrictions in that energy, and then travels through the system of the recipient.

Anyone can give reiki, but each individual needs attunement or initiation first in order to become fully open to the healing energy. The attunements are specific procedures which are based on sacred symbols and various techniques that are unique to reiki.

The attunements are carried out by reiki masters and increase the individual's capacity to allow a greater amount of universal life-force energy to pass through them. A channel is created in each attuned person, which enables the increased energy to flow freely. This source of universal energy is external and limitless by its nature.

Simply healing

Although reiki is a hands-on form of healing, no manipulation of the body is involved, as it is in therapies such as osteopathy, chiropractic, kinesiology, rolfing, massage, shiatsu, and reflexology. There is, therefore, no risk of injury, aches, or pains occurring after a reiki treatment, as there can be with some other therapies.

No substances are involved in the practice of reiki, as they are in homeopathy, herbalism, Bach Flower remedies, and aromatherapy, as well as in orthodox medicine.

Reiki can be used successfully in conjunction with other complementary therapies and healing forms, and with orthodox medical treatment.

For everyone

Reiki is not a religion and can therefore be practised by people of different faiths. Unlike some forms of healing, it has no specific religious dogma associated with it. Instead, reiki is about encouraging people to have trust in themselves and in the universe.

Accessing Love

Reiki can be defined as a network of love based on universal life energy. It is understood to be given and received in gratitude.

HOW REIKI WORKS
During treatments, reiki practitioners use specific hand positions that correspond to the physical body, its organs, and the seven chakras (see Giving a Treatment, pages 90–141). The chakras are centres of concentrated energy that vibrate over specific areas of the body. Reiki energy gently balances the chakras and the energy field that surrounds the body, as well as soothing physical and emotional complaints.

The seven chakras
Each chakra connects with particular glands and parts of the physical body, as well as specific aspects of emotional and spiritual energy, from the basic survival instinct to the quest for understanding.

2 *The sacral chakra relates to the gonads, reproductive organs, legs, and vitality.*

5 *The throat chakra relates to the thyroid, vocal cords, arms, hands, and self-expression.*

1 *The root chakra, at the base of the spine, connects to the adrenals, bladder, genitals, spine, and life force.*

3 *The solar plexus chakra connects to the pancreas, liver, and stomach, and power, fear, and control.*

6 *The third-eye chakra is associated with the pituitary, brow, intellect, and seeing, through the "third eye".*

4 *The heart chakra is associated with the thymus, heart, lungs, and love.*

7 *The crown chakra connects to the pineal gland, cranium, and spiritual consciousness.*

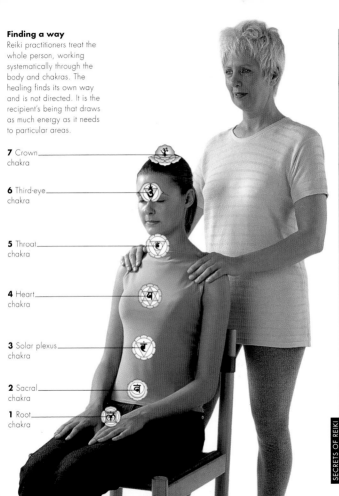

Finding a way

Reiki practitioners treat the whole person, working systematically through the body and chakras. The healing finds its own way and is not directed. It is the recipient's being that draws as much energy as it needs to particular areas.

7 Crown chakra

6 Third-eye chakra

5 Throat chakra

4 Heart chakra

3 Solar plexus chakra

2 Sacral chakra

1 Root chakra

How Reiki Helps

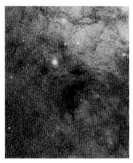

Finding our place
*Using reiki regularly can
help us to accept our place
within the universe.*

Reiki can provide a straightforward
and simple way of healing long-
term disorders and conditions.
Reiki is said to be particularly useful for
people suffering from medical
conditions that orthodox medicine often
can do little to cure, such as eczema,
asthma, allergy, headaches, migraines,
back pain, and arthritis.

All of these conditions are common
and widespread, yet can be
debilitating and depressing. Reiki

practitioners believe that these
conditions may simply be outer
symptoms of an inner dis-ease. They
may indicate a lack of balance and
blockages in the energy within the body
that reiki has the power to heal.

Reiki can also be used to provide
instant and immediate aid in cases of
shock. It may relieve the pain and
symptoms of injury, such as bruising,
and help to promote quicker healing.

As well as helping to ease physical
problems, practising reiki on yourself or
receiving reiki from a practitioner can
promote a sense of mental well-being
and help to relieve conditions arising
from modern living, such as stress.

A sense of belonging

Reiki also works on the emotional and
spiritual levels of our being, helping us
to put right what is wrong in our lives.
All of us need to acknowledge the
different levels of existence and
recognize that we are more than
practical beings who exist simply to
work, bring up children, and look after

our homes. As part of human life, we need to engage in relationships within the family, with partners, friends, and acquaintances, and with colleagues at work. We also may need or want to take part in the affairs and activities of our local community.

In order to be able to play a full role within life, we need to be and feel whole within ourselves. Reiki is said to be able to help with this, and this in its turn can also enable us to help others with their lives and be more compassionate towards those in difficulty or pain.

We all need love, security, balance, and a sense of belonging. Reiki practitioners and masters believe that reiki can offer us this. At its best, reiki can help us to find our place within the universe, helping us to foster a sense of trust and balance.

Accepting Life

Many of us feel the pain of not belonging, or not feeling right within the world. Reiki can help bring us to a place of acceptance.

THE POWER OF REIKI

Reiki masters and practitioners believe that reiki brings integration and order to your life and allows a change of consciousness. This enables new opportunities to develop and present themselves. It could be said that life is like walking a tightrope – and that reiki has power to steady us so that we acquire a sense of balance. It helps us, motivates us, and energizes our spirit. Some supporters regard reiki as a safety net for life, which we can use to support us on the journey from sickness to health, stress to relaxation, and difficulty to happiness or resolution.

In tune with the elements
The power of the natural world, which can be accessed through reiki healing, helps to sustain and revitalize the spirit.

Long way down

Without a spiritual aspect to our lives, existence can seem bleak. Reiki can provide a safety net.

Case History

George, 56, is a farm worker who had cancer of the stomach. He used reiki to help him cope with the symptoms and he has since fully recovered from the disease.

George was introduced to the practice of reiki in 1997 after having reflexology for stress and other ailments. In May 1998, his reiki practitioner advised him to visit his doctor for a stomach problem. George was diagnosed with cancer the following year, after months of tests. He received reiki treatments throughout this trying time, which helped him to relax and eased his tension and anxiety.

Both George and his wife attended a reiki course and practised on each other regularly. When he went for surgery, George felt completely relaxed and afterwards the first thing he asked his wife to do was to give him some reiki. From that day on, he has not looked back, and believes that his recovery from the operation was helped along by the many people who sent distant healing.

Discovering Reiki

Warming hands
*Once you have experienced
the healing touch of reiki, you
may decide to learn the
techniques for yourself.*

People come to reiki in many different ways and through many different routes. Some discover the power of reiki through receiving treatment from a professional reiki therapist; others may be given healing by a friend who has learned reiki. Some experience it for the first time while attending a course to learn the techniques for themselves.

You can receive reiki treatments without having to learn any techniques. However, many people progress to learning the techniques from a master.

This enables them to practise reiki healing on themselves and on others. Some may eventually work towards becoming a reiki master, although this requires a long-term commitment.

Reiki is becoming increasingly mainstream and therefore more widely known and publicized. However, many people first hear about it through friends or acquaintances, and this can often be an ideal way to find a therapist or a course that suits them.

At a time of need

You may have heard about reiki some time before you actually decide to have a treatment or to undertake a course of training to become a practitioner. On the other hand, you may have a treatment and decide there and then that this is the therapy for you. It is often said by practitioners that reiki appears in your life when you are in greatest need of it, or that it finds you just when your potential for healing has reached its highest level. Reiki can benefit everyone, and, because it does not involve any manipulation of the body, it is perfectly safe for the elderly, and for babies and young children. Reiki is also suitable for ill and disabled people, which other therapies may not be.

Case History

Dee, 38, is a dental nurse. She first received reiki more than ten years ago but began her training only recently.

She first heard about reiki from a reflexologist, who offered to do some healing on her knee, which was sore and swollen. She was sceptical but her knee improved straightaway. Even so, many years passed before Dee responded to that initial experience and took her first degree in reiki.

A couple of years ago Dee's hair began falling out. This was the third time she had had the problem, and it was worse than ever before – her doctor told her that it was stress-related and that she could go bald. Dee had learned more about reiki by that time and had heard of a weekend course in reiki.

The weekend proved to be a turning point for Dee. She received treatment with the focus on her bald areas, and left feeling a new energy and an inner calm. She was surprised to find that her hair started growing again within a week. Today she has a curly mop that grows at a normal rate, and she gives it reiki regularly to make sure that it stays that way.

The world over
Anyone can receive or learn reiki. Once you have learned it, you can send it to anyone in the world.

THE SIMPLICITY OF REIKI
Such is the accessibility of reiki that everyone, no matter who they are, what they do, or what their state of health, can receive it, learn it, and practise it. Reiki is not an academic subject to learn, and you do not need any special equipment in order to give the healing. All you need is a sincere commitment to help others and to help yourself to progress and develop.

Reiki for everyone
People who have learned reiki include teachers, builders, doctors, computer operators, farm workers, engineers, therapists, carers, and students. Even children can learn to give reiki and, because the techniques do not require any particular level of fitness or mobility, so too can the elderly and people who live with chronic illnesses.

Joan was in her 70s when she decided to train in reiki healing in order to treat herself.

Joan had a problem with frequent weeping from her left eye. The day after her reiki training class, Joan noticed that there were no tears in her eye. Several years later, her eye problem has not recurred. She also finds it hard to sleep at night and practises reiki on herself before bed. It helps her to relax, and although she doesn't sleep for long, she finds that the few hours' sleep she has are sound.

A place of calm

A Zen garden is built on the principle of simplicity, much like the reiki approach to healing.

The History of Reiki

Mountain air
*Reiki founder Dr. Usui discovered
his inspiration while meditating
on a holy mountain in Japan.*

Reiki came to the Western world via
California and Hawaii from Japan.
Reiki evolved from the experience
and dedication of Dr. Mikao Usui, a
Christian Professor of Theology at
Doshina University, who lived in Japan
in the nineteenth century.

Dr. Usui one day was asked a
question by one of his students which
he found himself unable to answer. The
question posed was, "How exactly did
Jesus heal?" Realizing that he could not
answer the question, Dr. Usui is said to

have understood that he had accepted
the beliefs of Christianity without
investigating them for himself. He
decided to leave his post and travel
and study in the hope that this would
help him to find the answer to the
student's question.

During his travels, Dr. Usui studied in
the United States of America, spending
seven years in Chicago and earning a
doctorate in scripture at university. Dr.
Usui eventually returned to Japan,
where he studied the ancient language
of Sanskrit, which has its origins in
India, and began reading the scriptures
of Japanese Buddhism.

The birth of reiki
While studying in a Buddhist monastery,
Dr. Usui is said to have come across a
manuscript containing a formula for
healing, represented by symbols. He
believed these symbols could reveal the
healing of spiritual leaders, such as
Jesus Christ and the Buddha. As
nobody in the monastery could explain
the symbols to him, he decided to

meditate on a holy mountain to see if he could discover the answer from within. On the twenty-first day, he is said to have experienced an expansion of consciousness that not only revealed the meaning of the symbols to him but left him with a heightened awareness and a capacity for healing himself and others.

A healing system

Dr. Usui spent the rest of his life healing the sick and troubled and teaching the healing system that he called "reiki". After some years, he came to believe that people needed to play an active part in their own healing if the effects were to be long lasting. He therefore also began teaching the five precepts of reiki. These aimed to help people foster a positive mental and spiritual attitude which complemented the healing (see pages 34–43).

Knowledge Lies Within You

"No man can reveal to you aught but that which already is half asleep in the dawning of your knowledge." Khalil Gilbran, *The Prophet*

All over the world

Originating in Japan, reiki has now spread throughout the world and continues to grow.

COMING TO THE WEST

Dr. Usui passed on his knowledge to Dr. Chujiro Hayashi, who set up a clinic in Tokyo. In 1935 a woman called Hawayo Takata, from Hawaii, visited the Tokyo clinic, where she received treatment for a tumour every day for eight months. Mrs. Takata became a dedicated student of reiki. After some years Dr. Hayashi initiated her, charging her with the responsibility of carrying on the tradition.

The next step

After Hawayo Takata had completed her long period of treatment and training, she returned to Hawaii. There, she devoted the rest of her life to practising and teaching reiki healing. By the time of her death in 1980, Mrs. Takata had trained 22 masters of reiki.

Tokyo

Continuing journey

The masters trained by
Hawayo Takata took reiki to
the United States of America
and Canada, and from there
to the rest of the world. All
reiki masters should be able
to trace back their reiki
lineage to Dr. Usui.

United States

Hawaii

The 22 reiki masters

- George Araki
- Dorothy Baba
- Ursula Baylow
- Rick Bockner
- Barbara Brown
- Fran Brown
- Patricia Ewing
- Phyllis Lei Furumoto
  (Takata's granddaughter)
- Beth Gray
- John Gray
- Iris Ishikuro

- Harry Kuboi
- Ethel Lombardi
- Barbara McCullough
- Mary McFadyen
- Paul Mitchell
- Bethel Phaigh
- Barbara Weber Ray
- Shinobu Saito
- Virginia Samdahl
- Wanja Twan
- Kay Yamashita
  (Takata's sister)

The Reiki Degrees

Reiki teaching is generally divided into three main levels in order to help those who are learning the practice to access the energy at a responsible pace. Level 3 is sometimes split into two stages, and is described as Level 3 and 4 in this book.

- Level 1 can be defined as hands-on healing for oneself or others.
- Level 2 is distant healing.
- Level 3, also known as Master's I, focuses on spiritual deepening.
- Level 4 is Master Teacher.

Reiki proponents believe that it is important to assimilate fully the teachings of each level before going on to explore the next. The journey through the reiki levels should be undertaken with guidance, care, and joy, so that understanding and consciousness can be developed, deepened, and strengthened gradually.

A lifelong commitment

The primary function of the first level of reiki is self-healing and self-development. However, it is also

1 Reiki is always with you
The foundations and principles of reiki are as solid and dependable as a rock.

possible to practise reiki on others, such as family and friends, after just one weekend of training by a reiki master.

Reiki could be said to be not so much taught as experienced by the student. The teacher gives each student four attunements, placing the sacred symbols in a certain order and in a certain way to balance the appropriate chakras (see pages 72–73). This involves a sacred ritual which is said to allow people to contact their own inner truth and spiritual dimension.

As well as being attuned, students learn the hand positions for self-healing and treating others, and discuss the responsibilities of being a student of healing. After training, practitioners are asked to continue with their own self-development. This may include going to regular support and practice groups and studying. Practising regular self-healing treatment after training helps to improve the flow of energy through the body, and is therefore thought to help students through the period of adjustment after the attunement.

Once students have assimilated and practised the teachings of Reiki 1 for a length of time, many go on to learn Reiki 2, which enables them to give distant healing to others. They may also decide to develop reiki further and become a master. Ideally, one should undergo a lengthy apprenticeship before taking this step. Reiki masters believe that becoming a master involves a lifelong commitment because of the role a master may play in helping others to change their lives.

2 To have and to hold
Making a commitment to the principles of reiki is a life-enhancing step forwards.

Learning Reiki

Reiki is its own teacher: the more we put into it, the more we will receive from it, and the more it is able to teach us.

3 Bird on a wing
Reiki understanding frees the individual to fulfil his potential and fly free, perhaps for the first time.

A new day
Reiki encourages us to start each day afresh, with a new way of viewing life.

THE REIKI PRECEPTS

Taking responsibility for your own life and your own healing is a vital part of the reiki philosophy. The five precepts of reiki were taught by Dr. Usui as reminders to help people aid their self-healing by adopting a positive mental attitude. He developed the precepts after he observed that the beggars he had treated had returned to living on the streets of Kyoto. This made him realize that people need to be more than simply passive recipients of a healing process if it is to have long-term results.

Do not worry
To release yourself from worry or anxiety is the first precept. Worry and anxiety are understandable human responses to various situations, but it is a fact that worry never improved any situation or exerted a positive influence over its outcome. Worry brings with it fear and blocks your emotions as well as your hopes for the future. It is helpful to think about what you can do, rather than what you can't. If you release yourself from even some of your worries, you will notice a growing sense of calm.

A Recipe for Positive Living

The five precepts of reiki are vital components of a fulfilled life and each one is intended to be followed on a daily basis. They encourage us to believe that even small steps can make a difference to our happiness and well-being. The precepts are produced here in the form of affirmations or reminders.

• Just for today, stop worrying: just for today, my mind is easy.

• Just for today, do not get angry: just for today, I am at peace.

• Earn an honest living: I earn my living honestly, doing no harm to anyone, or anything, nor harming the environment.

• Honour everyone you meet: I honour my parents, elders, teachers, children, friends, and myself.

• Show gratitude to every living thing: I give thanks to all living things and all situations, whatever they may be, for their valuable lessons in growth and understanding.

Stop worrying

Once we have learned to let go of worry and anxiety, we can use our energies to the full.

The effects of worry

When we are worried or anxious, our bodies produce a rush of adrenaline. This provides the energy for the basic survival acts of flight or fight. However, the way we live today means that we rarely need to use this energy, and it can do our bodies more harm than good. The short- and long-term effects of worry and anxiety include breathlessness, headaches, chronic stress, back pain, fatigue, digestive problems, and blocked arteries.

The Second Precept

Do not get angry
Reiki helps us to observe and tolerate the frustrations and difficulties of life without wasting energy in anger.

To release ourselves from anger is the second reiki precept, and for many people the most difficult. Most of us recognize that anger is destructive, negative, and exhausting, as well as being symptomatic of a lack of self-control. It makes sense, then, to learn to control your anger and to negotiate sensible outcomes to any conflicts. If you manage to stay calm, others will be more likely to respond constructively to you and difficult situations are less likely to escalate.

All disputes, however large or small, will have originated with anger and then spun out of control. Look at disputes between neighbours, physical violence, riots in the streets, and disputes between neighbouring countries and continents. War itself is a symptom of anger that has evaded resolution through diplomatic channels.

One must ask oneself what is achieved through anger. Generally, it is little more than a waste of energy that could be better directed elsewhere.

How to right the wrong

Anger at perceived injustices in the world may seem justifiable but, again, may ultimately achieve very little. A more useful response would be to try to right the wrong through constructive action and dialogue.

The reiki precepts encourage us to take each day at a time, which is a useful reminder. One of the most helpful things you can do is to decline to give way to anger today. If you try to do the same the next day, and the next, then positive action, dialogue, compromise, and negotiation are more likely to become a way of life.

Coping with anger

Declining to give way to anger may involve simply noticing and reflecting on it when it arises, rather than acting upon it. You can learn to release the accumulated negative energy that may lead to anger, or to channel the emotion, once you have noticed it, through vigorous exercise or hard physical work. Even housework can be used to release pentup emotion. Breathing exercises, yoga, meditation, or visualization may also help you to cope.

Once you have acquired good management of your anger, any stress-related conditions should begin to ease. Eventually, chronic stress should become a thing of the past.

A Way of Change

Reiki works as a vehicle for transformation – but we have to remember that changing ourselves is not always easy or rapid.

THE THIRD PRECEPT

To learn to honour your parents, elders, and teachers is the third fundamental principle of reiki. Our parents gave us life, and without them we would not be here in any sense – physically, mentally, emotionally. The third precept encourages us to learn from our parents, and from other elders, and to respect their wisdom. We can learn from them not only how to develop in ourselves the qualities that we like and respect in them but also how to modify any qualities that we do not like.

Respecting our teachers
A close relationship with a grandparent can help a child to realise how much he can learn from his elders. A broad spectrum of people can be seen as our teachers, and we encounter them from our earliest days of life, through to the school and college years, and onwards to our adult lives, with our bosses, colleagues, and our other relationships. All of the people we meet on our journey through life can be seen as having something to teach us or show us. It is up to us to have the humility to appreciate, to listen, to learn, and to understand what the lessons of life are.

A constant process
Learning from our elders forms an integral part of many human group structures, such as tribes or families. When we learn how to show gratitude for the teachings that we receive from others, we develop our own self-esteem and belief in ourselves – so that we too become able to pass on what we have learned from others.

The Fourth Precept

Earn an honest living
Self-respect is an essential element of a happy and fulfilled life: let your work be your fulfilment.

To be able to earn your living honestly and to do no harm to anyone, anything, or the environment is the fourth precept of reiki. Another facet of this precept is to respect those people who are making an honest and conscientious living. The nurse, the teacher, and the road sweeper all deserve our respect.

Many people gain a sense of identity and self-worth from their work. Some common causes of energy blockages, aches and pains, and recurrent minor ailments are destructive and negative emotions such as guilt, fear, unease, and a bad conscience. All of these can stem from feeling negative about your work. Stress too is a rising problem and one of the major causes for absence from work.

It is important to acknowledge the contribution you make through your work, however insignificant you feel it may be. Simply acknowledging at the start or end of each day the effort you put into your work can help to increase your sense of self-respect.

Discovering harmony

Most people know whether or not they are in the right employment or activity to help them express themselves and find self-esteem. The fourth precept encourages you to take the first steps to cleanse and rationalize your life. This may mean taking steps to change your career, such as retraining, or simply being open to new possibilities. You may not be in a position to change your work, but you can work on developing a positive attitude towards it and fulfilling your responsibilities in the best way you can. Remembering to start afresh with this each day will help you to focus on being positive.

In reiki, being truthful and honest is recognized as a fundamental principle for living. Adopting the precept of living honestly is an integral part of respecting others and yourself.

Case History

Julie is a 26-year-old mother looking after two small children at home. She uses the fourth precept to guide the way she connects with people throughout the day.

A modest person, Julie says she would like to be thought of as someone who does lots of little things for the good of others. As well as looking after her family, Julie looks in on her elderly neighbour every other day, helps to run the local Cub Scouts, and is a member of Amnesty International, a movement which campaigns for the welfare of political prisoners.

True to Yourself

Learn to accept yourself as you are and to recognize and acknowledge the value of your contribution to other people.

THE FIFTH PRECEPT

Showing gratitude to every living thing is the fifth principle of reiki. By giving thanks for all that we have, we help to expand our hearts and increase our sense of joy in life. This may mean showing our gratitude to others, giving thanks to the people who help us, and valuing the animals, plants, trees, and oxygen around us. It may even be something as simple as appreciating a beautiful sunset or a flower. Noticing all these things helps us to acknowledge that we are part of a larger world and reminds us to respect it.

Lend a hand
Helping others in need is a sure way to feel good about yourself. A small act of kindness brings its own reward.

The more love you give

Showing affection to a pet or working animal, such as a guide dog for the blind, is a way of offering appreciation for its presence in your daily life.

Being grateful

The fifth precept is to give gratitude to every living thing and every situation, whatever form it may take. This includes appreciating even the difficulties and challenges of life, since from them we can learn how to change, develop, and grow.

The Tradition of Exchange

Giving and receiving

Finding a way of giving thanks for a treatment helps to keep the energy moving between the recipient and the giver.

One of the traditions of reiki is that of exchange, in which one gives something in return for what one receives. This was initiated by Dr. Usui, the founder of reiki, to help ensure that recipients were playing an active part in their healing. Reiki practitioners do not charge for their services, unless they are professional therapists. However, it is usually appropriate to acknowledge a reiki treatment and give thanks with flowers or a small gift. Alternatively, people may give their services or time to help the reiki practitioner as a token of their appreciation. On a more spiritual level, the exchange could mean making a commitment to change and to renewed consciousness, in return for receiving the gift of healing energy.

Fees for reiki

Professional reiki therapists charge a fee for their services. This will vary depending on where you live and whom you see. Occasionally, someone will be treated free of charge or at a concessionary rate depending on his needs and his circumstances. Reiki practitioners traditionally treat their parents free of charge to acknowledge the fact that, as parents, they were responsible for the gift of life.

Fees for learning reiki techniques vary. Generally, reiki masters may require the equivalent of around two or three days' wages to study Level 1, around six or seven days' wages for Level 2, and two weeks' wages for Level 3. Mastership fees are usually discussed and negotiated individually with the master but may require a substantial commitment.

It is often possible to study reiki more cheaply than this. However, you should always ask about the credentials and lineage of the teacher before you sign up, to check he is able to provide what you need (see pages 68–69).

Case History

Susan, 35, is a shop manager. Recently she attended a reiki weekend course to learn the basic principles.

Since the reiki course, she has practised on herself often. She also offers reiki to her landlady, who often feels tired after spending a long day standing up at work. When their first session had finished, Susan's landlady told her she had rarely felt so relaxed and yet so full of life. Susan also benefited from the healing, and noticed that she, too, felt very relaxed afterwards. She was rewarded with a large chocolate bar and a bunch of flowers.

Your Commitment

Each level of reiki has an appropriate amount of exchange, which is enough to make people think about their level of commitment to it.

RECEIVING A TREATMENT

You are more likely to have a truly positive experience of reiki if you have no expectations and no preconceived ideas. Reiki practitioners encourage an open mind to treatment. In this way, you are unlikely to be disappointed. However, you may be surprised at the stirring of awareness and the beginnings of understanding. Physical aches and pains may disappear of their own accord as tense muscles start to relax, mental anguish starts to diminish, and solutions start to present themselves. The experience of reiki is different for each one of us, according to who we are and what our story is.

Finding a Practitioner

Asking around
The best way of finding a reiki practitioner is to ask your friends and contacts.

Y ou may have experienced reiki sessions with a friend or family member and feel you now want to explore reiki with a more experienced practitioner, or you may be new to the healing. Either way, if you are to invest time and money in sessions with a professional reiki therapist, it is worth spending some time seeking out someone who suits you.

You will be looking for someone whom you feel to be on the same wavelength as you. Above all, your reiki therapist should be someone whom you will be able to talk to easily and whom you can trust to help you progress in your development.

A personal recommendation from someone who knows you well is often the best way to find a good reiki therapist, but you can also get in touch with professional reiki organizations (see page 221) and ask them to recommend a practitioner in your area.

Checking credentials

Because the basic techniques of reiki are simple to learn and accessible to everyone, it is important to make sure the therapist has sufficient depth of experience. Professional reiki therapists should have completed at least level 2 and are likely to have an ongoing relationship with their own master.

You may like to ask her what her lineage is. All reiki practitioners should be able to trace back their teachings in a direct line to Dr. Usui (see pages 28–31) and be happy to explain how they are connected to the first masters.

The therapist's journey

It is also useful to know how long the therapist has spent exploring reiki and progressing through the levels – this can be a useful indication of how seriously she takes the healing. Some people complete all three levels in a weekend course. Most reiki masters feel that this does not allow sufficient time for the necessary understanding and spiritual development to grow.

Other therapies

Reiki can be used in conjunction with other complementary therapies, and some reiki therapists practise other therapies such as shiatsu, crystal healing, or colour therapy. It is worth making it clear before the treatment that you want to receive only reiki healing, if that is the case.

Safe Practice

Although reiki is safe and suitable for everyone, a professional reiki practitioner should have insurance to treat clients and students at her practice.

WHAT TO LOOK FOR

A good reiki therapist will have many of the personal qualities that you look for in a reiki master (see pages 68–69). She should be friendly and open but professional and respecting of confidentiality. You want – and need – someone who will be sensitive to your needs and who is willing to answer any questions you might have about the healing. Above all, you want to feel comfortable about talking over any life issues you might have and to know that your therapist has sufficient experience and knowledge to help you.

Good communication
Try to speak to the reiki therapist before going for your first session. Most professional therapists will be happy to talk to you by phone, or meet you in person before a treatment, and this is an excellent way to check that you will feel at ease. If you feel anxious, it can be a good idea to take a friend along. It is also a good opportunity to check what the fees for treatment will be.

A healing place

Although you can receive reiki anywhere, a professional therapist will probably have a room where she treats patients. Because reiki involves accessing energetic forces, the room should be clean and free from clutter. Check that it is quiet and offers enough privacy.

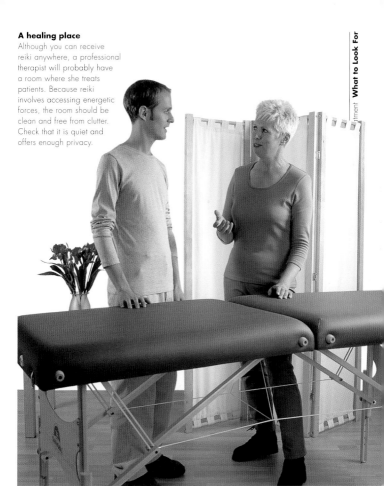

A Time and Place for Treatments

From the heart

As the universal life force, reiki is in our hearts and all around us. Its healing can be accessed anywhere and at any time.

You can have a reiki treatment anywhere at all. Once you have learned the techniques, you can treat yourself at home, outside in the open air, on the bus, or in a car. You do not need to make any special arrangements for a treatment. However, if you are having full reiki sessions, it is well worth investing some time to make sure that you get the most out of them.

Making space

For a full reiki session, scheduling is all important. Sessions usually last between 45 minutes and an hour, though sometimes a treatment may be longer. You will be much more likely to benefit from the session if you have set aside sufficient time and are not worrying, for example, about an appointment or picking up your children from school.

You may wish to build in a few moments for quiet reflection before the treatment starts. It may help to make sure that you arrive five or ten minutes early so that you have to wait for your appointment rather than rushing in the minute you arrive. You should also give yourself a little time afterwards to give you the chance to feel and assimilate the effects. If at all possible, try not to plan too many activities for the day on which you receive a treatment.

You can also help to make the most of reiki through choosing the right therapist for you, making sure that the

surroundings are suitable, and
preparing and calming your mind so
that it is open to receiving the healing
(see pages 56–57).

Case History

Reiki is the first thing Helen, 53, a company
secretary, turns to when she needs to help
others. Much to the amusement of her family
and friends, she finds herself with "hands on"
in the oddest places.

On a skiing holiday Helen was relaxing in a
bar when she spotted a fellow skier with his leg
propped on a stool after a fall. She offered to
help, placing her hands over the injured area.
On another occasion, in a shopping mall, Helen
laid her hands on a woman's chest after she
had had a prolonged coughing fit.

Although she knows how helpful a quick reiki
can be, Helen makes sure she has a few
minutes to herself before and after visiting her
practitioner, to help access her inner calm
and fully experience the effects of the healing.

Facilitating Reiki

With reiki treatment you can experience an
awakening of consciousness. You can respect
its power by giving it time and space.

A blue mood
*Even the simplest items – a glass
bowl with beads – add a
touch of beauty to your home.*

LETTING ENERGY IN
If possible, spend some time before treatment in an environment that emanates peace. If you are having a treatment at home, it is worth trying to create a space that is healing. Buildings acquire atmosphere by soaking up the energy around them. The more positive the things that happen in a room, the better it feels to be there. A tranquil atmosphere enhances the pleasure of reiki, and a safe haven provides an excellent space for treating yourself, or for promoting your well-being.

Healing Space

Consider all these factors to help create an atmosphere that is conducive to healing:

- bright and soft colours
- freedom from clutter
- fresh air
- space near the windows
- warmth
- quiet

Let in the light
*Simple touches can make a
basic room beautiful. First,
allow the sun to shine in.*

A room with a view
*Nature is a joy to behold,
whatever the season, even
when you're inside.*

Let the wind sing
*Wind chimes placed around
the house provide an on-off
symphony of harmonious tones.*

Lie back and relax
*Big, colourful cushions make
even the simplest of rooms
more luxurious and comfortable.*

Preparing Yourself for a Treatment

Inner cleansing
Washing away the cares of the day will help you to relax into a reiki treatment.

In order to experience fully a reiki treatment, you need to make space. You need enough physical space so that you do not feel hemmed in, and you need to create a sense of mental space, to allow any expansion of the mind or dawning of consciousness to take place. Going into a treatment with an open mind is the most important thing you can do.

Setting aside worries

Reiki practitioners believe that you will not be able to make the most of the reiki experience if you are worried about lots of other things at the same time. You need to set aside time – and worries – in order for reiki to do its healing work. Simply making the decision not to worry for an hour or so will help you to lose yourself in the reiki experience for as long as it lasts and enable you to soak up the energy that it creates for you.

Take a few minutes before the session to sit and breathe quietly, or to meditate (see pages 168–69). This will help you to feel centred.

What to wear

Wear comfortable clothing that is not restricting in any way, so that you can relax properly into the session. Don't forget the temperature of the room: as we lie still our body temperature cools, and it is therefore important that the room be warm enough. Take an extra, loose-fitting sweater with you, to put on if you get cold. You will usually be asked to take off your shoes, belt, and spectacles if you wear them. Practitioners also recommend that you remove your watch or any jewellery before a treatment.

Simple hygiene

Reiki practitioners will generally wash their hands before giving a treatment. If you are the receiver, it is a natural courtesy to have had a bath or shower, and washed your hair before your meeting. Provided that you eat healthily, well, and regularly, you are unlikely to suffer with bad breath problems, but many people like to clean their teeth before a session too.

Quiet Time

Help your understanding to deepen by sitting quietly and still for a short period before reiki. Focus on feeling and opening your heart.

The world opens up
Your first reiki may reveal new vistas, new challenges, and new opportunities to you.

YOUR FIRST EXPERIENCE
You may find that your first reiki treatment is life changing. But it may not be what you expect. People's reactions to their first experience of reiki vary widely, from bemusement to serenity, elation, and joyfulness. Sometimes there is a profound emotional release, characterized by sobbing and a sensation of being reborn. The gift of reiki is its ability to relax and heal, so whatever your initial reaction, be reassured that you have embarked on a positive journey.

Profound relaxation
Some people find themselves wanting to sleep after reiki. This is a common reaction.

A new awareness

Reiki can open up whole new areas of consciousness, as you tune in to more vibratory realms.

Case History

David, 61, wanted reiki to help a bad back, but found the treatment had a profound emotional effect on him. He could scarcely walk up the path, and his back was so painful that he had to have reiki treatment in a seated position.

After five minutes' treatment, his body began to shake. He was racked with sobs for the next 40 minutes. His practitioner talked quietly to him and then continued with the session. When it had finished, David admitted that he felt he had been waiting to let out that pain for more than 40 years.

David's sobs have lessened at each session. He looks younger and a lot more relaxed, and says he's beginning to put life into perspective. His back pains are also improving.

Initial Reactions

Emotional reaction
One's first experience of reiki may produce sorrow, grief, apathy, or great joy, release, and relief.

Your first reactions to a reiki treatment may be seen during the treatment itself, or they may take hours, even days to appear. That is not uncommon. Some people experience an emotional backlash – they may find that they are upset, irritable, and weepy. Alternatively, they may manifest certain physical symptoms, including hot flushes, nausea, or headaches. All these are quite normal responses, and most people will find that they pass reasonably quickly.

Reiki often balances out bodily functions, so you may notice more frequent urination and more regular bowel movements. These are positive signs of improved energy flow. Some people also find that a reiki treatment helps them to rediscover the ability to sleep properly, even if they have suffered from insomnia for many years.

A healing response

After a treatment, you may experience what is known by some practitioners as a healing response, and by others as a healing crisis. In this, the person may temporarily feel much worse than she did before the treatment.

This is normally a relatively short phase and afterwards can be seen as a rebalancing and centring of a disturbed energy force. This phase can be painful and unsettling, but it usually settles within a few hours or the next day at most. However, it is one of the reasons why it is helpful to make some time to rest and relax in a quiet place after receiving a treatment.

Integration

Many people experience a sense of release, calm, and peace both during and after a treatment. Some characterize this as a feeling of "coming home to oneself", or of uniting the mind, body, and spirit.

Case History

Gilly is a 40-year-old journalist who started having reiki sessions to help her deal with irritable bowel syndrome (IBS).

Gilly found great peace during the first treatment, but physically felt quite poorly, and very cold and shivery afterwards. Her IBS became worse for about a week, and it was about three weeks before she started to feel better. Since then, Gilly has noticed a real improvement, and the treatments have also helped to release her hip and back, which were very stiff. Gilly has also developed a calmer outlook on life which enables her to cope when times are hard. She feels that she is sustained by "something", and believes that that something is reiki.

Being Open

Reiki practitioners believe that learning to be open and acknowledging how little one truly knows are the first steps to wisdom.

Long-term relationship
*Making the decision to commit
to regular sessions can lead to
a lifelong connection with reiki.*

MAKING A COMMITMENT

It is not always easy to integrate reiki into a busy life, and it may mean setting aside leisure activities, rearranging your schedule, or enlisting the support of family members or friends. However, if you want to experience the full effect of reiki, it is worth committing to regular treatments. Having an occasional treatment can be helpful, but the effect of successive treatments will be far stronger. Your therapist may ask you to come weekly, particularly for the first few sessions.

The cost of reiki

The cost of a reiki session varies, and some therapists may offer a cheaper rate to those in need. However, having regular reiki treatments will require a financial commitment. You may need to consider how reiki features as a priority in your life – do you really need, for example, a new car or a new washing machine? Would that money be better invested in reiki?

The road to healing
*However busy or stressful the
pace of modern life, making time
for reiki will prove worth it in terms
of relaxation and healing.*

Welcoming the dawn

Regular reiki may help you to feel an increasing sense of joy as you greet the day.

Time wise

You may think you have no time for reiki, but the treatments will help you to prioritize and make the most of the time that you do have.

Developing Effects

Deepening sensitivity
Your intuition, your feelings, and tolerance for others all deepen and strengthen with reiki.

As you have regular reiki treatments, you may notice significant shifts in your attitudes towards and experience of life. Reiki practitioners say that successive treatments help you to develop a clearer perspective and a more relaxed attitude towards those around you.

Many people gradually become aware that their trust in the universe is strengthening, that their relationships are more rewarding, and that their physical health and well-being improve.

The intuitive sense

As you progress on the reiki journey, you may become more sensitive. Many people notice an improvement in the five senses: vision, taste, smell, touch, and hearing. Colours may seem brighter, sounds more intense, and tastes and smells stronger, for example.

Many people notice that their intuitive sense, sometimes known as the sixth sense, also grows as they continue to receive treatments. For example, you may become more aware of what people are leaving unsaid and more sensitive to what cannot be expressed or can hardly be felt.

These developments are not always comfortable. With increased sensitivity can come increased vulnerability, and you may need to make sure that you take time for yourself each day to assimilate what is happening.

Decision making

As your intuition grows, you may feel a greater sense of ease around making decisions and discover a new ability to trust your inner voice or conviction. This may help you to have confidence that you are making the right decisions for your particular situation. Because the healing emphasizes a sense of trust in the universe, many people start to experience less worry about their decisions and have a calmer attitude to the possible outcomes.

Spiritual deepening

For some people, the development of a sense of trust in life leads to an emergence, or a deepening of spiritual conviction, which can take many different forms.

Developing awareness brings with it greater knowledge about the effects of your actions, and thus a greater sense of responsibility. Reiki practitioners say that this is yours to take on with confidence and integrity.

Receiving What You Need

People will respond differently to reiki, and the healing they receive will vary depending on their needs at the time and their openness.

HOW DO I LEARN REIKI?

People usually learn the techniques of reiki during a formal course taught by a reiki master, often over the course of a weekend. Reiki practitioners claim that people are often drawn to learning reiki at a time when they most need the relaxation and healing that reiki can offer. ❧ However you discover reiki, any reiki master or practitioner can tell you that the exploration and discovery is a long and worthwhile journey. One continues to learn day to day, week to week, for many years after taking that first step.

How to Find a Course

Ask your therapist
A personal recommendation is ideal when you are looking for a reiki course to join.

Some reiki masters offer to teach levels 1, 2, and 3 during a single weekend course. However, most masters agree that this does not allow time for a student's energies to settle, his healing abilities to progress, and his understanding to grow.

Speed does not enhance the process of learning reiki and developing one's focus and healing. Rather, it may produce strong responses in the student, which may cause him to become uncomfortable and confused.

Where to look

If you are receiving treatments from a reiki therapist and have built up a good relationship with him, he is probably the best person to ask about reiki courses. He may run courses himself or be able to recommend a master who does. Alternatively, you may hear of a course from a friend who has learned reiki. Professional reiki associations (see page 221) will be able to put you in touch with a master in or near your area. Some associations have introduced a teaching qualification to help clarify suitability of courses.

Guidance and support

The changes brought about through learning reiki are powerful, but an experienced master can guide, support, and advise you. Take some time to assess the master's experience, simplicity, and commitment. Personal rapport with a master is essential, but you should also look at how the course is structured and whether the class size and surroundings feel suitable for you.

Course Checklist

You may like to ask the master the following questions before committing to a course:

• How many people do you usually have in a class?

• Where do you hold your classes?

• How long does each class last?

• Which levels do you teach?

• How long have you been practising?

• Are you a member of any professional reiki organization?

• What is the name of your master? And the name of his master? This helps you to check that the master knows his spiritual lineage.

Qualities of a Master

These are the qualities you may like to look for in a reiki master:

• personal rapport;

• ability to communicate;

• confidentiality;

• professionalism;

• challenging outlook;

• warmth;

• joyfulness.

WHAT TO EXPECT

Reiki courses will vary in content, depending on the master teaching them. However, most are taught informally, and balance practical work with theory, including the history and traditions of reiki, how it works, and the benefits it may bring. All students will be attuned to the appropriate level (see following pages) and shown how to work with reiki energy. The reiki master will also talk to students about the possible effects that learning each level of reiki may bring.

Sharing experiences

A class may consist of up to 12 people. Different people's responses and experiences, and the group's social contact, can benefit everyone's learning.

Most of the teaching is done verbally

Close your eyes and
feel the energy flow

Focus your attention
on the hands

Learning to heal

*An important part of the course
is learning how to give others
the healing energy of reiki.*

Time to talk

Many reiki masters will
include self-development
exercises in a reiki course.
These help students to
build up a sense of trust
towards the master and
other students. There is
usually plenty of time for
students to raise concerns
with the master.

The Attunements

Unlocking the door
*The attunements act as an
initiation and enable the student
to access reiki healing.*

chakras, the seven centres of energy in
the body (see pages 18–19), invoking
the symbols and silently repeating the
mantras. This is said to create an
energetic vibration that helps balance
and realign the chakras and alter the
flow of the body's energy.

Because healing energy is universal
and all around us, each person already
has a connection to it. The attunements
work to enhance this existing
connection and create permanent
access to the life-force energy.

A sacred ritual

The attunements serve as an initiation
process, and are commonly regarded
as a sharing between the master and
the student. They are usually respected
as a sacred ritual.

The different ways in which
individuals experience attunements can
vary from feelings of peace and joy to
seeing a spectrum of colours. Some
people simply experience a sense of
relief or release, or may connect to a
feeling of general well-being and

The reiki attunements serve to
realign the student's energies, to
enable him to access the infinite
supply of reiki energy. The reiki master
attunes each student individually, using
the sacred symbols discovered by Dr.
Usui (see pages 28–29), and specific
mantras, or sound vibrations, that
represent the symbols.

The student usually sits down and
closes his eyes while the master attunes
him in silence. He works on the

harmony. These attunements are an essential part of reiki and signify a major difference between reiki and all other forms of healing.

What the attunements do

There are four attunements for first degree, one for second degree, and one for master's degree. Each is intended to work on progressively higher levels of the inner being.

Once the student has received the first attunements, which work on the physical body, healing energy can be drawn down through the top of the reiki practitioner's head, through the heart, into the solar plexus, and out through the hands. This enables him to use the healing energy on himself or others. The more advanced attunements work on the mental, emotional, and spiritual levels. All bring balance and harmony.

The Beginning of Truth

First one door opens... then another... and another... and another... on each person's journey towards enlightenment.

LEVEL 1 CLASS

The level 1 class introduces the reiki student to the basic techniques of giving reiki and includes the first four attunements. The main focus for learning reiki 1 should be to develop and to heal oneself. The course will also enable you to offer reiki to others, such as your friends or your family, but it will not equip you with the necessary skills and experience to be a practitioner.

Let your whole body relax and de-stress

Rest your hands in the positions for two minutes

Anywhere you like
If you can't lie full length, you can treat yourself sitting comfortably upright like this.

Allow yourself to heal
Once you have learned the techniques, you will be able to give yourself a full treatment.

Make sure the
receiver is seated
comfortably

The master will answer
any queries you have
about the treatment

Touch is all-important
in reiki; it can be used
to soothe the receiver

Working together

A reiki course gives the ideal
opportunity to practise reiki
on yourself and also on other
students. This is a practical
way of introducing you to
the power of reiki and can
help each participant to
benefit from the healing
energy during the course.

Level 1: Learning to Heal

Universal energy
Once you have received the level 1 attunements, you open up a gateway to life energy.

The first degree, or level 1, is usually taught over a single weekend. Students are taught the history and theory of reiki and shown the basic techniques they need to treat themselves and others.

The student receives four attunements, which create a strengthened connection between the individual and the life-force energy. Receiving the attunements is an essential part of the course, and enables the student to access and use this energy for healing.

The attunements

The four attunements for Level 1 awaken and amplify the life-force energy. They allow an increased flow of this energy to travel through that person's being. The attunements are focused on the four higher chakras – the crown (seventh), third-eye (sixth), throat (fifth), and heart (fourth). They mainly work on opening up the body, so that the student can become a recipient and giver of life-force energy.

Many masters space out the attunements, giving one attunement in each half-day session. This gives the student time to absorb what he is learning and feeling.

Practice and sharing

Part of the course will focus on self-awareness and sharing experiences in the group. This helps people to relax and feel comfortable. Students will learn how to give a full body treatment to themselves and others and will have an opportunity to practise the correct reiki touch and hand positions. The master will explain the etiquette of giving reiki and help students explore the responsibilities of healing. (See Giving a Treatment, pages 90–141.)

Changes and effects

The course should cover the changes that you or others may experience after the attunements. Most masters agree that the first 21 days after attunements are an important time, and you may notice significant life changes. Some people experience physical symptoms, such as colds, thought to signify a healing or cleansing process. You may choose to detoxify or scale down activities during this time.

After the attunements, many people notice a heat emanating from their hands as they treat. Sometimes there is also a tingling or pulsating. All these are signs that healing energy is flowing.

Your Energy

After your attunements, you may start to become aware of magical changes in the strength and flow of your energies.

No limits
With reiki, you can send healing, loving energy anywhere in the world.

LEVEL 2 CLASS
The essence of level 2 reiki is distant healing, which enables you to send reiki to someone or something not present. This requires considerable focus. Learning level 2 reiki is also essential for those wishing to become a reiki practitioner (see pages 194–97). It is usually recommended that students allow some months to elapse between attaining and practising level 1 and embarking on level 2.

Concentrate on feeling the energy moving out through your hands

Distant healing
You will learn how to send reiki to someone who is close to you, no matter where he is.

Holding a loved-one's image can help to make you feel closer to her

Wish you were here
When someone you care about is absent, looking at a photograph while you send distant reiki helps to make the experience more profound.

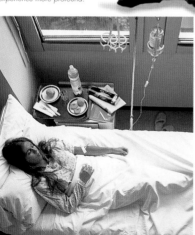

Love across the miles
You can receive reiki healing whenever you are in need, even if the giver is far away.

Level 2: Deeper Healing

Coming together
Learning distant healing means that you have a direct line to help loved ones, wherever they are in the world.

The second degree of reiki is usually taught, like the first, over the course of two days. Again most of the teaching is verbal. In level 2, students are introduced to three reiki symbols and shown how they can be used in the healing.

There is a single attunement, given by the master to each individual student. The attunement is intended to give you access to the power and meaning of the symbols and add to the strength of reiki healing.

Sacred symbols

Because the reiki symbols are sacred, they always remain confidential. They are revealed only to those people who have taken second-degree reiki and have received personally the attunement that empowers them.

Accessing level 2

Self-awareness exercises and the sharing of experiences and life stories play a significant part in the course. A discussion of the reasons for wanting to progress from level 1 to level 2 is an essential part of the process. Reiki masters and practitioners usually say that once a student is sufficiently tuned and in touch to be able to describe level 1, he is ready to embark on his attunement for level 2.

While level 1 works on the physical and energetic body, level 2 brings the focus to the mental and emotional levels. You learn techniques for allowing people to heal in their own way and for dealing with the emotional releases that can occur when people receive reiki.

You will also learn techniques for healing in a group and for distant healing. This enables you to send healing to people who are not present, to buildings and places, and to the less tangible aspects of life, such as situations, journeys, and relationships. (See pages 180–83).

Case History

Jan, 38, was transferred to her company's overseas branch soon after taking reiki level 2.

Family difficulties led Jan to offer distant healing to people who could no longer come to her for help. This was a strange experience for Jan but helped her to cope with what had seemed insurmountable problems. Instead of worrying about people at home, she focused on sending them reiki. Was it merely coincidence that a young relative who had lost a sense of purpose became motivated, or that the cousin who was in conflict with her sister-in-law was suddenly moved to phone to ask how she was? Jan believes that positive reiki energy was responsible.

The Sacred Way

A good teacher will be happy to show direction to the honest and self-confident pupil, and guide him along the way.

Deeper sensitivity
*As we progress through
the levels of reiki, we
become more attuned
to the world around us.*

LEVEL 3 CLASS
The third level of reiki is for those who decide to bring reiki fully into their lives and wish to devote themselves to giving and receiving reiki healing. Many masters say that you need to have a strong sense of vocation to take the third degree, as it involves a commitment to spiritual development and requires a deepening of trust in the universal energy. There is just one attunement for this level. This is received alone in a ritual one-to-one sharing between master and student.

Blossoming in the desert
*A barren, arid landscape will
flourish and bloom under the right
conditions. Let reiki inspire you.*

From a seedling
Our understanding of reiki grows stage by stage, ripening into a solid foundation for living.

You and the universe
Feel your connection with the earth and the universe: mentally affirm this feeling over and over.

Level 3: Mastership

Reiki at its highest level
*Becoming a reiki master is
one of the most profound and
important life achievements
for many people.*

Level 3 is the first stage of becoming a master, with level 4 the final stage. Originally, there were only three levels, and many masters still adhere to this system. However, others feel that dividing this higher level into two stages can enhance and broaden the student's understanding. Level 3 is used to focus on the individual's own spiritual development, while level 4 concentrates on teaching people how to teach and help others through the reiki levels.

Some people attain level 3 but do not wish to progress to teaching, while others enjoy taking on the responsibility of initiating and teaching others.

The training
Because becoming a reiki master involves focusing on spiritual growth, you will usually be taught on a one-to-one basis. This means the master can tailor the course to your needs.

Becoming a reiki master usually involves developing a close relationship with a master and working alongside him over a period of some months or years. Because this level requires a lengthy apprenticeship, it usually demands a high level of financial, spiritual, and emotional commitment from the student (see pages 44–45).

Any teaching reiki master can initiate other masters, but it is recommended that he has been a practising master for three years before doing so. Some masters do not comply with this and may therefore have little to offer the serious student of reiki.

The attunement

There is a single attunement for level 3, which works on opening up the spiritual and most profound level of being. It marks a shift from the ego and self to a feeling of oneness with the universal life-force energy.

The attunement is usually given during a one- or two-day course. This includes reviews of the student's past experiences of reiki and discussion of his reasons for wanting to attain this higher level. Meditations and breathing exercises may also be taught.

The attunement is given by the teaching master, using the fourth sacred symbol and its accompanying mantra. Students are taught the mantra, and the attunement usually takes place in an individual ritual, perhaps in a sacred place that has significance for both student and master.

Transformation

"The attunement was like a bolt of energy through my body. I recognized it as something deep on all levels of my being." Reiki master

Into the future
Those who study level 4 prepare to journey into the very core of their being.

LEVEL 4
The highest level that you can study in reiki is level 4, the master teaching level. It continues the mastership process begun in level 3 and equips you for teaching others and giving attunements at all levels. Reiki mastership is not something that you can acquire over a weekend. This may take months, even years, and requires a close, trusting relationship with your master. Being a reiki master is an ongoing process, and those who complete level 4 often see themselves as apprentices on a pathway to self-realization.

Reiki master
Angela Robertshaw has been a master for many years. She derives deep fulfilment from the many people she has healed and feels reiki has strengthened her connection with the world.

Level 4: Becoming a Teaching Master

Dedication and sensitivity
In order to train as a reiki teaching master, you will need above all an awareness of others' feelings.

The purpose of level 4 reiki is to train teaching masters. The final attunement is given in level 3, and so this level focuses on the practical techniques for teaching and initiating other reiki students. The student is shown the master symbol and taught how to use it to attune others.

Reiki masters agree that reiki becomes central to their lives. Teaching requires a sense of responsibility, humility, and an unshakeable respect for reiki and for the students. As a teaching master, you become a guardian of the reiki tradition. You also need to be available for people when they need you for guidance. This can require considerable time and commitment.

The training

As with level 3, this final level is taught on an individual basis. You are likely to continue working alongside your reiki master, assisting him on reiki courses, giving attunements, and helping to set up sharing groups.

Your master may train you in an informal way, during his own courses, or set aside specific days to explain how to structure a class, how to support students and how to perform attunements. You may have a natural ability to teach, but some formal qualification is often thought desirable.

You and your master will decide when you are ready to run courses on your own. Usually, you will organize and teach a level 1 and level 2 course under his guidance and supervision, before he gives you his approval to begin teaching alone. However, even once you are ready to teach, you are likely to continue an ongoing relationship with your master.

An awareness of others

A reiki master is not a guru and is not considered to be better than other people. The hallmarks of mastership are integrity and equality. A master assumes responsibility for changing people's consciousness, and with this gift come responsibilities. He will need to make a real commitment, to show discipline and dedication in his practice, humility at all times, intuition and imagination, and a generosity of spirit.

Mastery is Humility

The easiest path does not always lead to the greatest understanding, but as your understanding grows, so will your conviction.

GIVING A TREATMENT

There is great joy in giving as well as in receiving a reiki treatment. As you lay your hands upon the receiver, you may feel a rush of energy, a tingling, or a warm sensation in your hands or other parts of your body. You may feel calmer or more balanced after giving a treatment, which can last as long as one-and-a-half hours or be as short as a few minutes. With reiki you always treat the whole person rather than any symptoms that may be mentioned, allowing the reiki energy to find its own way. The treatment may be hands-on or hands-off. The receiver should remain fully clothed except for shoes and spectacles.

Reiki Etiquette

Simple hygiene
*Clean hands, short nails, and
no rings or other jewellery clear
your hands for the passage
of reiki to the receiver.*

There is an etiquette that should be observed during a reiki treatment. Some of the following guidelines are part of the reiki tradition, and others are simply good manners.

Communication
Never offer someone a treatment more than three times. If your offer is not accepted by then, leave the person alone, and trust that she will ask when and if she is ready to receive your help.

Check with your receiver whether the treatment is to be hands-on or hands-off, and ask if she has any tender areas.

Explain that the receiver can stop the treatment at any time, although it is better that the treatment continue without interruption if possible. Before starting to treat, ask for permission to touch the person (see box opposite).

Hygiene
Make sure that your nails are reasonably short and that you have no ragged cuticles that may scratch. Always wash your hands before giving a treatment, making sure that your fingernails are clean. If you have long hair, tie it back so that it cannot fall into the face of the receiver.

Do not smoke before treating, as your hair and clothes will be permeated with the smell of tobacco smoke. Try to leave 24 hours between eating spicy or garlicky foods and giving a treatment. Clean your teeth, and if you have any doubts about the freshness of your breath, use a breath-freshening spray.

A quiet atmosphere

Make sure that the room is clean and aired before you start a treatment session. Burn incense or scented candles if necessary.

Put on your answerphone, and turn down the ringer on the telephone. Switch off your mobile phone, if you have one, and remind the receiver to do the same.

If there are other people in the house, hang a "Do Not Disturb" notice on the door of the room in which you are giving the treatment, or warn them not to come in.

Drinking water

Have a bottle or jug of water and two glasses in the room. Both giver and receiver should drink water before and after a treatment, to help to expel toxins from the body.

Permission to Touch

Some receivers may be a little apprehensive. A simple, sincere request for permission to touch helps them to relax into the treatment.

A hint of rose
Rose petals floating in a bowl of water provide the most subtle of natural fragrances.

A GOOD ENVIRONMENT

You do not need to treat in a place that has been decorated in any particular way. However, a tranquil environment that is clear of clutter and contains beautiful things will help to make people feel cared for and nurtured.

Scented blooms

Fresh-looking foliage

A living world
Plants and fresh flowers are a quick and easy way to bring life to a room and add vibrancy to a dull corner. However, make sure that you look after plants well, and change the flowers once they start to die, as few things are less conducive to a healing atmosphere than wilting foliage or flowers.

Inviting glow
Lots of candles placed around a room give a welcoming feel, the flames providing invitation and warmth.

Universal elements
Some people like to consider the balance of energy in the room where they treat and include all the elements of the universe: wood, water, fire (light), metal, and air. A room that reflects the balance of all these elements creates harmony, which may help you to connect more easily with the flow of energy.

Creating a restful space
One or two beautiful items in a room draw the attention and provide an ambient resting place for the gaze.

A Healing Room

Natural elements
The atmosphere of the practice room is all-important – you need to create a healing, peaceful space for the receiver.

Reiki healing is best done in a peaceful atmosphere. If you are going to treat at home, choose the quietest room in the house, well away from any traffic noise. You may like to close the curtains, as this will reduce noise from outside. Carpeting and soft furnishings, such as sofas, will also absorb external sound.

Give some thought to the quality of the air. You may wish to invest in a humidifier if the atmosphere is very dry,

a dehumidifer if it is damp, or an ionizer to clear the air. Incense, scented candles, or an aromatherapy oil burner may all help you to create a pleasant, healing atmosphere.

Don't forget the temperature of the room, which should be warm enough to keep both giver and receiver comfortable. The recipient's body temperature will drop when she lies still for any length of time, so make sure there is some form of heating in the room that can be switched on during the treatment if necessary.

Check that there is enough light in the room. Lamps provide a more subtle, pleasing effect than central fixtures. The colours you choose are important, too – a mixture of warm colours, such as gold or deep red, and soothing shades, such as green and cream, would be ideal.

What you need

Any reiki practitioner will tell you that in material terms you need nothing in particular to give or receive reiki. But you do need to make sure that the

recipient is comfortable and that you are not straining while you treat. Ideally, the recipient is lying down and the therapist is neither stooping down nor reaching up during the treatment.

A practice couch (massage table) is ideal for giving reiki since the legs can be adjusted to make it the appropriate height for the giver. However, you can use a couch or single divan bed rather than a formal practice table. Alternatively, the recipient can lie on folded blankets on the floor.

If you find it hard to stand for any length of time, buy a mobile stool, such as those hairdressers sometimes use. This will enable you to move around freely but stay seated.

Case History

Jan, a florist, has been giving reiki treatments to friends for seven years. She takes special trouble to decorate and use her smallest bedroom as the "reiki room", and to make sure it is always kept clean and tidy. Her best friend always asks to stay in this room when she comes for an overnight visit since that is where she says she sleeps best.

A gentle touch

Apply a lotion to soften the hands, then loosen the fingers by pulling from knuckles to tips.

FOCUSING
Before you give a treatment, take a few moments to steady and centre yourself and to focus your energy flow. Stand with your shoulders completely relaxed. Stretch upwards your upper body and neck while breathing in, and then exhale, allowing the shoulders to drop. Pay attention to your hands, which are central to the healing. These exercises and massage techniques will help to keep them supple.

Flexible fingers

Curl fingers inwards to palms, starting with little finger, ending with thumb. Uncurl and repeat.

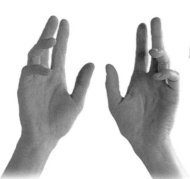

Preparing your hands

With the thumb, make gentle but firm circles from nails to knuckles, up to the wrist.

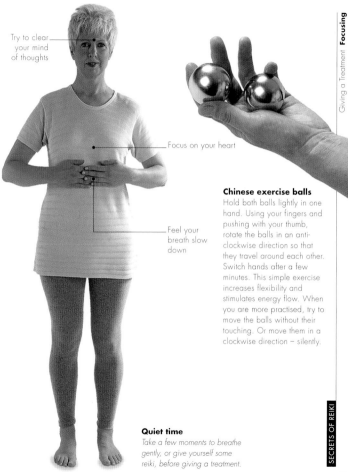

Try to clear your mind of thoughts

Focus on your heart

Feel your breath slow down

Chinese exercise balls

Hold both balls lightly in one hand. Using your fingers and pushing with your thumb, rotate the balls in an anti-clockwise direction so that they travel around each other. Switch hands after a few minutes. This simple exercise increases flexibility and stimulates energy flow. When you are more practised, try to move the balls without their touching. Or move them in a clockwise direction – silently.

Quiet time

Take a few moments to breathe gently, or give yourself some reiki, before giving a treatment.

The Reiki Touch

Hands that heal
*The light touch of caring hands
can provide a sense of comfort
and solace to those in need.*

The touch of the reiki practitioner is important since most treatments are given hands-on. However, a hands-off treatment is also an option for people who dislike being touched or who may be either too tender or infectious to be touched.

Always check with the receiver whether she would prefer a hands-on or a hands-off treatment since some people may be too shy to request it. If a recipient does want a hands-off treatment, use the same positions as those described on the following pages, but keep your hands a short distance above the body.

Gentle energy

Hold your hands with the fingers together and your wrists relaxed. Breathe smoothly and deeply: the energy will flow through your body more easily if you are relaxed.

Make your touch gentle without being timid. Take care not to spoil the treatment by pressing hard with your hands or letting them hover. Let your hands rest gently on the body.

The touch required is very different from the touch of massage or the touch of manipulation, both of which are much firmer than reiki. Unlike these forms of treatment, reiki does not seek to bring about a physical reaction.

As a practitioner, it is crucial that your touch be considered and focused, out of respect for the recipient and to allow the healing energy to be transferred. If your attention drifts, bring it gently back to your hands.

The first touch could be a soft stroke of the hairline, rather than immediately placing the hands on the head. This is a gentle way of making a connection, of establishing the important initial physical contact.

The importance of touch

We all need physical contact that is caring, non-sexual, and non-aggressive. Many people feel starved of touch and of the comfort and reassurance that it brings. In times of distress or pain, touch is usually the instinctive reaction when we want to help.

Parents instinctively place a hand on a sick child's head, or cuddle a crying baby. Whether rubbing a sore part of our body or holding the hand of someone in distress, we use touch in our life without being aware of it. Reiki is a more focused extension of loving touch.

Caring for Yourself

Healing does not always mean curing. Reiki is concerned with restoring a wholeness of spirit, whereby the receiver starts to heal from within.

THE 27 REIKI HAND POSITIONS

The full reiki treatment comprises 27 positions, illustrated from this page through to page 125. These positions are for use on someone lying down, but most can also be used on a seated person (see pages 130–31). A full treatment takes between one and one-and-a-half hours, depending on the time available and the receiver's comfort. In the case of a child, you may want to give a shorter treatment or ask her to sit rather than lie down.

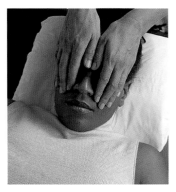

Eyes
1 *Place your hands gently over the receiver's eyes, and let them rest there for 3 to 5 minutes.*

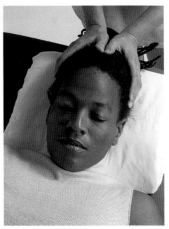

Crown of head
2 *Place your hands over the crown of the receiver's head for 3 to 5 minutes.*

How long for healing?

Suggested timings are given for each position but you can vary these according to the needs of the receiver and spend longer on areas giving pain or discomfort. Any sensations of heat or tingling in your hands can be useful indicators of when to move your hands to a new position: they may become more intense when the need for healing is greater, and lessen once the receiver has drawn sufficient energy.

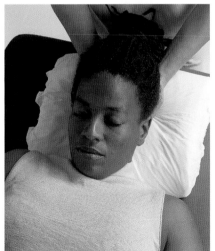

Jawline

3 Place your hands on the receiver's jawline for 2 minutes, or longer if she has dental problems and is in pain.

Back of head

4 Place your cupped hands under the back of the receiver's head for 3 to 5 minutes.

The Significance of Hand Positions 1 to 4

Confident and gentle

Many people feel protective of their face and may prefer hands-off healing here.

I t is usual to start a treatment with the head and face. These are particularly significant parts of the body in reiki because they are such sensitive areas, both physically and emotionally. Clearly, they also have a strong connection with our brain and mental energy. For instance, the eye area is the seat of the will and of clairvoyance. Here, perhaps more than anywhere else, your touch needs to be gentle.

1 Over the eyes

This is one of the seven main chakra areas (see pages 18–19), the third-eye chakra. It relates to the pituitary gland, which relates to most of the major functions of the body. This position can be used to treat sinus problems, colds, eye disorders, and stress.

This area is the person's intuitive centre and governs how she sees the world. Here reiki can bring clarity and insights to the receiver by taking her sight inwards. Treat this area for between three and five minutes.

2 Over crown of head

This is the crown chakra. It relates to the pineal gland, which regulates the hormones. Treatment here can be used to combat stress and memory problems and to regulate brain function.

Here, reiki can put us in touch with our spiritual self and help to lead us on our way to spiritual enlightenment. Treat this area for three to five minutes.

3 Jawline

Tension in the jaw may indicate a blockage of emotional and verbal communication. Any fear of expression may also be located here. Reiki is useful here for its ability to facilitate communication, gradually to break down emotional blockages around the jawline, and generally to refresh the energy channels. Treat this area of the body for about two minutes.

4 Under back of head

This position can be used to treat headaches, digestive disorders, and eye problems, as well as exhaustion and anxiety. Thoughts and emotions are believed to come together in this area. Reiki here helps to unite body, mind, and spirit. Treat for three to five minutes.

The Right Time

Reiki energy will find its own level. It is not strictly necessary to go through all the hand positions on the body during each session.

HAND POSITIONS 5–8 Suggested timings

are given for each position. You can lengthen or shorten these according to need. If, for example, the person has a sore throat or a cold, spend a longer time around the throat and a shorter time on the other positions. This is a good time to check that the treatment room is still warm enough for the receiver.

Ears

5 *Place your cupped hands over the receiver's ears. Let them remain there for 2 minutes, or a little longer if the receiver has complained of specific ear problems or earache.*

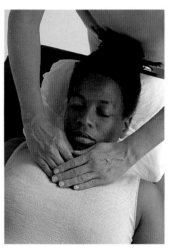

Throat

6 *Place your hands gently over the receiver's throat, taking care not actually to touch the throat, as this may feel threatening. Let the hands rest in this position for between 3 and 5 minutes.*

Heart

7 Place your hands on the receiver's heart. Let them rest there lightly for between 3 and 5 minutes.

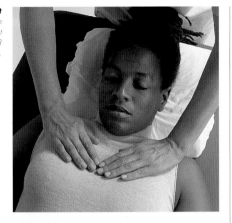

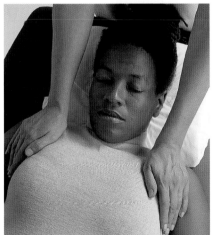

Armpit

8 Place your hands on (not under) the receiver's armpits. Rest them there for 2 minutes.

The Significance of Hand Positions 5 to 8

Loving communication
Reiki is believed to be able to clear illnesses produced from a lack of trust, caused by bad experiences in the past.

These areas, like the first four positions, all relate to highly sensitive and emotional parts of the body. They are connected with love, communication, and expression.

5 Ears

The energy points on the ears relate to every area of the body. The simple cupping position over the ears has been found to reduce ear problems such as tinnitus, and even to repair the nerve damage that sometimes causes deafness. Treating this position takes the sense of hearing inwards to enhance the receiver's inner awareness. Reiki here helps to amplify the receiver's inner voice in order to reduce the impact of outward stimulation. You can treat this area of the body for two minutes.

6 Throat

This is the fifth of the seven chakra areas (see pages 18–19). This position can be used to treat thyroid problems and high blood pressure. The throat and jawline are areas of expression and communication. You can treat this area for three to five minutes.

7 Heart

The fourth of the seven chakra areas is traditionally regarded as the seat of love and emotion. This position also governs the immune system and can be used to treat heart problems. Reiki on the heart allows it to warm, to soften, and to open, in time giving the receiver increased confidence and ability to trust. The whole chest area is concerned with relationships, matters of the heart, respiration, and circulation. Treat for three to five minutes.

8 Armpits

Placing the hands on the soft part of the receiver's shoulder towards the underarm allows the universal life-force energy to pass into the receiver's lymph system. This can have an energizing effect. The arms, regarded as extensions of the heart area, have some of the same significance as position 7, above. You should treat this area for about two minutes.

Changing Your Life

Reiki can cause a shift in consciousness that can last for the rest of your life. Some receivers note a distinctly positive change in themselves.

HAND POSITIONS 9–13 When the front of
the body is treated, powerful emotions are sometimes released by the receiver.
These are quite natural and should be regarded as part of the healing. Always
allow the receiver to express her emotions, while providing a quiet, soothing
presence that reassures her until her equilibrium is naturally restored.

Liver

9 *Place your hands side by side, fingers
together, on the area of the receiver's liver.
Rest them in that position for 3 to 5 minutes.*

Spleen

10 *On the other side of the body, place your
hands on the area of the receiver's spleen.
Remain in that position for 3 to 5 minutes.*

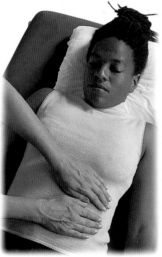

Waist

11 *Place your hands at the receiver's waist, as shown in the photograph, and let them rest lightly in this position for 2 minutes.*

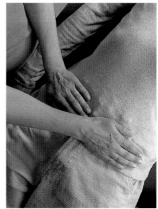

Lower abdomen – male

12 *Place your hands on the male receiver's lower abdominal area, but take care not to place them too near the genital area. Let your hands remain there for 3 to 5 minutes.*

Lower abdomen – female

13 *Place your hands on the female receiver's lower abdominal area, again, not positioned too near the genital area. Let them remain in that position for 3 to 5 minutes.*

The Significance of Hand Positions 9 to 13

Locating the problem
Reiki always finds its own level, so it will automatically find its way to any problem areas.

These positions are powerful areas to treat because they are concerned with gut reactions, fear, power, and the beginning of new life.

9 Liver and 10 Spleen

The liver and spleen relate to the third of the seven chakra areas (see pages 18–19). Working in these areas allows energy to be drawn into the receiver's liver, spleen, lungs, and stomach. All these help to enliven the digestive and elimination processes. You may notice that the receiver's breathing becomes more open, deeper, and more relaxed when you are treating here, while the stomach may rumble loudly.

This area relates to the solar plexus chakra and is the intuitive centre where we experience a gut reaction to a situation. Such reactions could include pain, fear, excitement, anticipation, ecstasy, or agony. This is the area concerned with issues of power and emotional control. Treat these positions for three to five minutes each.

11 Waist

The waist also connects to the solar plexus chakra (see above). Treat this position for two minutes.

12 Lower abdomen (men)

This is the second of the seven main chakra areas (see pages 18–19), which is associated with our vitality. It is

important not to place your hands too near the genital area since this may make the receiver feel nervous and uncomfortable. It is a simple matter of respect and courtesy. You can treat this area for three to five minutes.

13 Lower abdomen (women)

Again, this is connected to the second of the seven chakra areas, associated with vitality. Reiki, just like water, always finds its own level. If there are problems in the genital or reproductive areas, reiki will go to the healing priorities. These could include menstrual problems, difficulties in giving birth, and urinary tract problems, for example. You can treat this position for three to five minutes, but remember to be careful where you are placing your hands.

Loving Each Human Being

"When I feel whole it is easy to love myself and then I can love each human being for being the same as me." A reiki receiver

HAND POSITIONS 14–17

Some of our deepest-seated emotions and tensions are stored in the legs, in both the upper and lower areas, as well as in the knees. This is hardly surprising, since the legs carry the whole weight of the body. Reiki can release the underlying tensions, and the receiver may find herself able to take a step forwards in a new direction, feeling a renewed and often stronger connection with the earth. Both the back and the front of the legs should be treated.

Thighs
14 *Place one hand on each of the receiver's thighs, as shown. Let them rest in this position for about 2 minutes.*

Knees
15 *Place one of your hands on each of the receiver's knees, as shown. Let your hands remain in this position for 3 to 5 minutes.*

Calves

16 Place both your hands on the receiver's calves, as shown. Remain in this position for about 2 minutes.

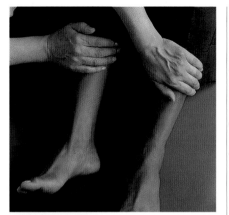

Ankles

17 Gently place your hands around the receiver's ankles, as shown, for 3 to 5 minutes.

The Significance of Hand Positions 14 to 17

Striding ahead

Deep-seated fears and old tensions often reside in the legs. Reiki can clear them away.

These positions, when worked one after the other, are good for active sports players. The treatment is also beneficial for the elderly who may, over the years, have developed an emotional build-up around the knees and the ankles, causing stiffness.

Some masters do not include the legs in their teaching programmes. Others, however, feel that the legs are an essential part of our being, as the means with which we move forwards and with which we connect ourselves to the earth that we inhabit. The relationship between our legs and their placement on the earth is an important part of our experience of rooting and centring.

14 Thighs

This is the area of the receiver's personal strength. Trust in one's own abilities is found here, as well as, sometimes, a fear of inadequate strength for the tasks that lie ahead of us. It is important that these areas be worked in order to restore strength, self-esteem, and self-belief. You can treat for two minutes.

15 Knees

This is the area where many fears can lodge themselves. These include the fear of physical death, fear of death of the old self, or ego, and fear of change. Treatment here equips the

receiver to face and even welcome
new challenges. Treat this position for
between three and five minutes.

16 Calves

This is the area that enables movement
towards goals. At the same time, it is
also the area where energy blockages
can represent a fear of action. It is a
good position to treat if you perceive
that inactivity is caused by blocked
energy. Treat for two minutes.

17 Ankles

The ankles represent our means of
balance and are therefore an important
part of the body to treat. You can treat
for three to five minutes, and longer if
you perceive there to be an element
of unsteadiness in the receiver.

Growing in Awareness

Moving forwards is an affirmation of life itself
and a sign of a newly developing awareness.
Reiki can help those who feel stuck to feel freer.

HAND POSITIONS 18–22

You will need to ask the receiver to turn over and lie on her front at this point so that you can treat the back positions. So many people complain of tension in the shoulders and back that it is hardly surprising to find that a great deal of stress and old negative emotions are lodged in these areas. Many practitioners say that they are often asked to focus specifically on the back.

Left shoulder

18 Place one hand on the receiver's shoulder muscle and the other over the shoulder blade, as shown. Hold for 3 to 5 minutes.

Right shoulder

19 Place one hand on the receiver's shoulder muscle and the other over the shoulder blade, as shown. Hold for 3 to 5 minutes.

Back

20 *Place your hands on the back, as shown, and hold the position for 3 to 5 minutes.*

Back

21 *Place your hands lower on the back, as shown, and hold the position for 3 to 5 minutes.*

Base of the spine

22 *Place your hands side by side, as shown, and hold the position for 3 to 5 minutes.*

The Significance of Hand Positions 18 to 22

Weight of the world
Blocked emotions and heavy responsibilities are all carried in the shoulders.

The shoulders and the back are without doubt the areas where we carry our worries, responsibilities, and all our unconscious tensions. Most of the people you encounter are likely to need reiki treatment for these areas. You can help the receiver to take in energy, to break down energy blockages, and to absorb the new-found energy of the life force.

Discharging anger

Reiki practitioners believe that the shoulders are where we carry the burden of life. It is said to be common for past memories to come to the surface during treatment of position 18 and position 19. These long-distant memories may cause changes to the breathing pattern and even crying or sobbing. A certain amount of pent-up anger and frustration may now be revealed and discharged.

Unseen tensions

Back problems are the one of the most common causes of people having to take time off work every year. It is here, according to reiki beliefs, that we store all of our unconscious emotions and excess tension. The junction between the lower and upper body movement may be particularly vulnerable. While women tend to store any tension in their shoulders, men are more likely to store their emotions in the belly, and this often produces problems in the lower back area. You can treat all these positions for three to five minutes.

18 Left shoulder

Here is where we are said to carry the burden of our mother's expectations.

19 Right shoulder

This is where we carry the burden of our father's expectations of us.

20/21 Back

Much of our emotional baggage is stored in the back, particularly in the lower part of the back.

22 Base of the spine

Treatment here can help energy to move more easily up the spine.

Help for the Workers

These hand positions also treat the kidney area: linked with anxiety, the kidneys are the most hard-working organs in the body.

HAND POSITIONS 23–27

We naturally feel safer and more protected when we lie on our fronts, and contained in that state of security we sometimes open up and allow our most profound emotions to rise to the surface. In this condition, healing can take place at a deeper than usual level, resulting in feelings of great calmness and relaxation. It is most important that the recipient feel totally at ease for this treatment.

Hips
23 *Place your hands to the side of the hip, as shown, and hold each side for 2 to 3 minutes.*

Thighs
24 *Place your hands on the back of each thigh, and hold the position for 2 minutes.*

Knees
25 *Place your hands on the backs of the knees, and hold the position for 3 minutes.*

Calves
26 *Place your hands on the back of each calf, and hold the position for 2 minutes.*

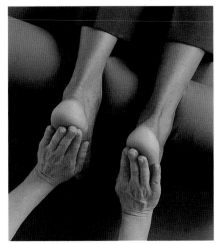

Soles of the feet
27 *Place your hands on the soles of the feet, and hold the position for 3 to 5 minutes.*

The Significance of Reiki Positions 23 to 27

Feeling grounded
*The hips, legs, and feet
literally keep us in touch with
the world. It is good to feel
a strong connection.*

Yanswer have seen how important the
leg positions are to aiding
forward movement, in the
physical, emotional, and metaphorical
senses (see pages 114–17). Now that
you are treating the back of the body,
rather than the front, you can reinforce
and recharge the energy flow that was
stimulated during treatment of positions
14 to 17. What you do here, with
positions 23 to 27, complements and

extends that work, helping the receiver
in her progression. These positions lead
on to the wake-up routine.

23 Hips

Many childhood emotions are lodged
here, as well as digestive problems and
arthritis. Treat for two or three minutes.

24 Thighs

Many issues with fear are contained in
this area. You can treat for two minutes.

25 Knees

These complex joints take a lot of strain,
and symbolize fear of taking a step
forwards in life. Treat for three minutes.

26 Calves

Working here for two minutes or more
helps the receiver to feel grounded.

27 Soles of feet

It is said that the feet contain energy
points that relate to every organ of the

body. Treat them for three to five minutes, or longer. Their treatment helps to reinforce the treatment of all the other areas of the body.

Wake-up routines

Once you have completed a treatment, which may have lasted from ten minutes for quick reiki, to an hour or one-and-a-half hours for the full reiki treatment, you should slowly and gently withdraw from the receiver and allow her a few moments in which to collect herself.

Some people may be sleepy, some may be invigorated, others may find themselves in a state of emotional release and need some time in which to feel at one with themselves. It is important that you perform the wake-up routines at the end of the treatment.

In Step

Every step you take brings you closer to the universal life-force energy, the dawning of enlightenment. Reiki helps you to take the steps.

WAKE-UP ROUTINES

Some people are in a state of deep relaxation after a treatment. The purpose of the wake-up routines after the completion of the treatment is to centre and ground the receiver, who needs to come back to reality and full physical and mental awareness. When you have carried out the routine on one leg or arm, repeat the process on the other.

1 *Gently lift the lower leg. Do not hold the ankle, but support the leg gently with one hand. Don't lift the leg too high (in case of back problems). Rotate the foot with your other hand, holding it from below.*

2 *Replace the leg. With both hands, gently squeeze (don't pinch) the leg three times, moving rhythmically towards the trunk of the receiver's body.*

3 *Stroke towards the buttock from the ankle three times. With a slight downward pressure, stroke back towards the ankle three times.*

4 *Shake out the arm. Avoid holding the wrist. Massage the hand and the fingers, working downwards from the wrist. Do this facing, and slightly to one side of, the receiver.*

5 *Squeeze with one hand from the wrist, up the arm and onto the shoulder three times.*

6 *Stroke from the wrist up to the shoulder three times. Keep your hand relaxed and follow the contours of the arm.*

7 *Stroke down the centre of the back, running the fingers down either side of the spine, not on it. Then, rub all over the back gently. Lastly, hold both your hands just over (not on) the neck, then the base of the spine for a few seconds each.*

Modifying a Reiki Treatment

Staying with the flow

By scanning the client with her hands, the therapist may detect some areas of imbalance.

In certain circumstances, you may need to modify the full reiki treatment, described on the previous pages. With quick reiki treatments, for example, you will need to focus on certain parts of the body and leave out others because of the restricted time available to you (see pages 132–33). However, you can be effective and helpful with just ten to fifteen minutes spent on giving energy to the receiver.

Seated positions

If you are in an office or another public place where it is inappropriate or difficult for the recipient to lie down, it may be best to treat her in a seated position. It is also often easier to treat children if they are sitting rather than lying down, as well as the elderly, who may have difficulty getting onto a couch or find it uncomfortable. Pregnant women may also prefer to receive a treatment when they are sitting. (See pages 130–31.)

In an emergency

With emergency reiki (see pages 134–35), you are likely to focus on one or two positions. If someone has a recent injury or burn, or is infectious, use your judgment when offering a treatment, and never assume it can be a replacement for medical intervention.

To avoid making a condition worse, and especially if there is an open wound, give a hands-off treatment.

Here, you hold your hands a few
centimetres or an inch above the body,
directly over the site of the injury.

When you can't help

There are some situations in which it
will be inappropriate to give even a
modified treatment (see box below), or
when your help is not welcomed. In
such cases, it is wisest to accept the
situation with grace.

Saying No

Even if you are asked to give a reiki treatment,
bear in mind that treatment may not be
appropriate for the following people:

• Any child without a parent or guardian
present to give her consent;

• Anyone who has been diagnosed with
severe mental or emotional problems,
unless a third party is present;

• Anyone who appears to have a vested
interest in remaining ill, or who you feel does
not really wish to become better;

• Anyone with whom you feel uneasy, even if
it is for no apparent reason.

GIVING SEATED REIKI

It is sometimes appropriate to treat someone in a seated position rather than lying full length on a practice table or bed. This is perfectly simple, although you will not be able to reach some areas of the body directly. You can, however, spend longer on the arms and hands, the head, neck and shoulders, and the knees and feet. Remember, reiki finds its own level and will heal where it is needed.

Focus on
your hands

Relax the
shoulders

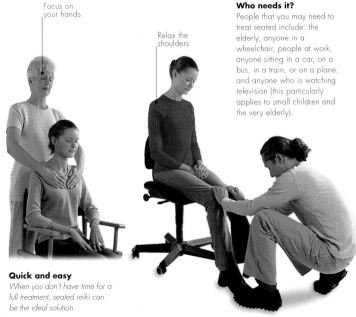

Who needs it?

People that you may need to treat seated include: the elderly, anyone in a wheelchair, people at work, anyone sitting in a car, on a bus, in a train, or on a plane, and anyone who is watching television (this particularly applies to small children and the very elderly).

Quick and easy

When you don't have time for a full treatment, seated reiki can be the ideal solution.

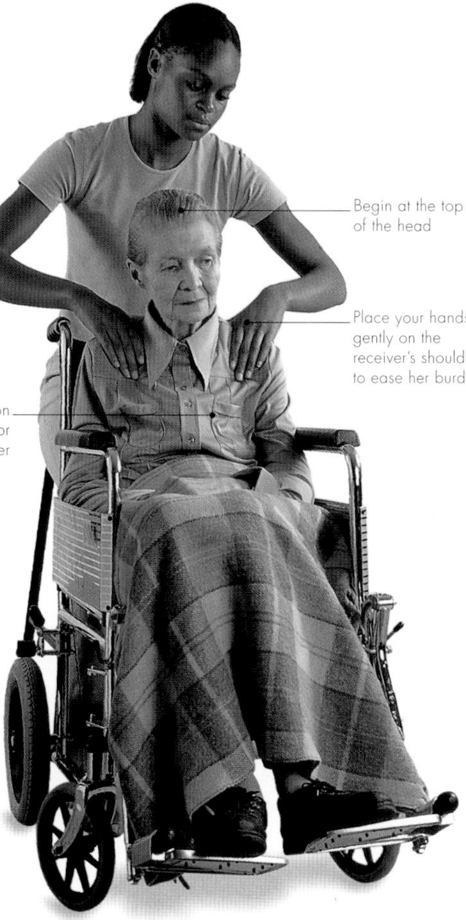

Begin at the top
of the head

Place your hands
gently on the
receiver's shoulders,
to ease her burden

Place both hands on
the receiver's heart for
3 minutes or longer

Quick Treatments

A mini reiki

Quick reiki may be just what babies need for colic, grumps, and teething problems.

Relaxing and refreshing

A short treatment is an excellent way to soothe anxiety or tension. You may find one helpful after getting out of the car after a long drive, before or after a long meeting or an important interview, or before or after exams.

The recipient should either lie or sit down comfortably. Place one hand over the solar plexus chakra, and the other hand below, so that it is touching the stomach. Simply hold for about ten minutes. This works equally well as a self-treatment or for helping others.

There may be many situations in which you would like to give a quick reiki treatment, when the situation is not one of emergency but simply a matter of lack of time. Quick treatments are equally suitable for yourself or for others.

It is perfectly possible to offer quick treatment wherever you see that it is needed: at work, in a shop, in the supermarket, on a train, or at an airport, for example.

Soothing to sleep

If you have trouble sleeping, a 15-minute treatment before bedtime each night can make all the difference between a bad night's sleep and a good night's sleep.

Lie in your usual sleeping position, on your back or on your side. Place one hand on your forehead and the other on your stomach. Allow the hand on your stomach to rise and fall in time with your breathing. Remain breathing

steadily for 10 to 15 minutes.
Gradually you should feel relaxed
enough to fall into a deep sleep.

Children, who tend to wriggle, can
be treated easily while they are
sleeping. Give hands-off reiki so you
don't wake them and be sure to check
with their parents or guardians first.

Case History

Anna, 32, is an office administrator who
works for a large computer company. She
found reiki the ideal treatment for a migraine
that developed after a four-hour meeting in a
hot and airless room. A sympathetic colleague
offered her a quick reiki, which she accepted
despite having never heard of the healing. The
colleague simply held one hand on Anna's
brow and the other on the back of her head
for about 20 minutes. Afterwards, Anna had
the same sensation that she remembered after
coming round from an anaesthetic – a sense
of relaxation and timelessness. Her migraine
was gone, although she usually finds they last
for 24 hours or more.

Some Is Better than None

One hour of reiki is better than 30 minutes
and 30 minutes is better than 15. But 15 is
better than 5. And 5 is better than none.

An unexpected shock
A sudden emotional upset can be soothed by an emergency reiki treatment.

EMERGENCY AND FIRST AID
You can give reiki treatments in all sorts of emergency situations. These include emergency medical and first-aid situations, and sudden emotional crises. Reiki is used in this context as a valuable relaxing and healing therapy which is complementary to medical treatment rather than an alternative to it, and for on-the-spot treatment after minor accidents or injuries.

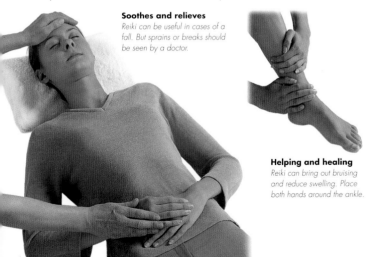

Soothes and relieves
Reiki can be useful in cases of a fall. But sprains or breaks should be seen by a doctor.

Helping and healing
Reiki can bring out bruising and reduce swelling. Place both hands around the ankle.

Case History

Mel's mother, Jean, arrived at her house unexpectedly one night, just after Mel had completed level 1 reiki.

Jean had trapped her fingers in the door of her car. She had a deep, bruised cut from which blood was pouring, and she was feeling very faint and tearful. Mel washed Jean's hand in cold water and gave it reiki. The bleeding stopped almost immediately, and Jean soon felt able to drive home. That evening, she visited her local surgery. The nurse told her that the healing process had already begun and that there was no need for stitches. At once Jean phoned Mel to thank her for the reiki.

A healing hug
Small accidents and upsets can often be soothed and eased by a few moments of reiki healing.

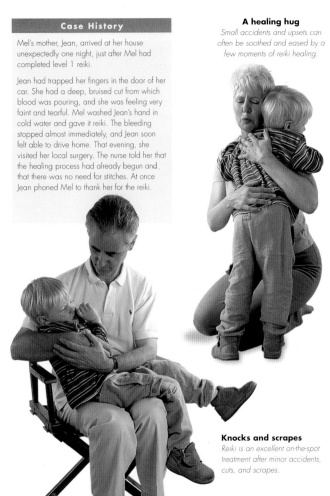

Knocks and scrapes
Reiki is an excellent on-the-spot treatment after minor accidents, cuts, and scrapes.

The Benefits of Treating Yourself

Convenience reiki

Deal quickly and easily with any physical or emotional problem by treating yourself to reiki – anytime, anywhere.

The busy lives that many of us lead can involve all kinds of stresses and problems. These may not seem significant enough to seek treatment from a practitioner but may gradually sap our energy and cause sleep or anxiety problems.

Reiki can help us to cope with continuing family problems, illnesses, and pain, which many of us have to tolerate. Treating ourselves is one of the simplest ways to alleviate difficulty and enhance well-being.

Developing understanding

Treating yourself on a regular basis will help to create a sense of wholeness and an understanding of the power of the universe. For many people the reiki experience enhances their understanding of their own belief system, whatever it may be. For many, reiki helps to put them in touch with the spiritual part of their being for the first time and increases their sense of belonging and tranquillity.

Physical well-being

On a physical plane, all sorts of pains and aches, such as a nagging headache or backache, may be relieved by treating yourself with reiki during a quiet moment in the day. Chronic ailments and disorders may be soothed by regular treatment.

Depression, anxiety, and other nervous and emotional conditions often respond well. Debilitating and negative belief systems, leading to poor self-esteem, may also gradually be resolved through the regular use of reiki, as the life-force energy seeps slowly into the psyche.

Do-It-Yourself Benefits

The benefits of treating yourself are chiefly:

• Developing and deepening your relationship with reiki energy;

• Encouraging your energy flow;

• Providing a quick pick-me-up when your energy levels are low;

• The timing – you choose when you treat yourself and for how long;

• Convenience – you simply do it at home or at work, without any need for appointments;

• Money – there is no charge, of course.

A Constant Companion

Open your mind and your heart, and reiki will find its way to help you out through the day and through the night.

Making time for reiki
You may wish to bring reiki into your day to give you the energy and strength to cope with life.

TREATING YOURSELF
You can reiki yourself every day if you wish: you will benefit from this by developing reiki as a force within you and developing your own energy channels. Reiki your whole body, not forgetting hips, legs, knees, and feet, whenever you have time, or concentrate on problem areas for a quick treatment.

1 *Place your hands over your eyes, with the palms over your face. Keep your fingers closed. Hold for 3 minutes.*

2 *Place your hands on your crown for 3 minutes.*

3 *Cup your fingers around your neck, with fingers closed, for between 2 and 3 minutes.*

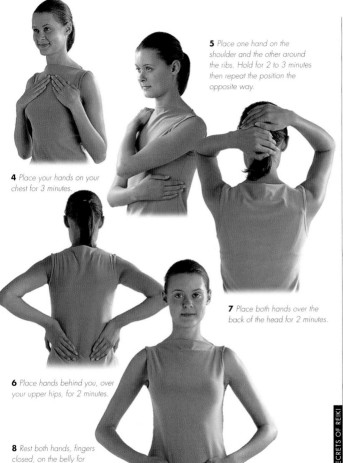

5 Place one hand on the shoulder and the other around the ribs. Hold for 2 to 3 minutes then repeat the position the opposite way.

4 Place your hands on your chest for 3 minutes.

7 Place both hands over the back of the head for 2 minutes.

6 Place hands behind you, over your upper hips, for 2 minutes.

8 Rest both hands, fingers closed, on the belly for between 2 and 3 minutes.

The Hidden Benefits

The hidden benefits
Just as the oyster yields its precious jewel, so reiki rewards the giver as well as the receiver.

The person who receives reiki derives many diverse benefits, be they emotional, spiritual, physical, or entirely transforming (see pages 144–55). But this is only part of what reiki does. Reiki is said to exert a powerful influence upon the giver, who may receive many hidden benefits.

You may feel calmer, more centred, and more alert after giving a treatment. As you focus on another person, you may feel your mind clear. In helping to make time and space for others, you may create the effect of making mental space for yourself, too.

Natural meditation

When you give a reiki treatment, you will find that it has a quietly meditative effect. Reiki is protective of the giver in that as the positive energy flows, it moves out through the giver's hands. There is no flow from receiver to giver, so you will not pick up any negative energies or symptoms from the receiver when giving a treatment.

In order to facilitate the flow of universal energy, it is important that the reiki giver, as well as the receiver, drink plenty of water throughout the day of the treatment (see page 157).

Gentle well-being

Reiki practitioners say that there is an accumulative benefit from giving reiki. Each treatment leaves a welcome and beneficial residue, which produces a feeling of well-being.

The giving helps you to connect with reiki energy and deepen your understanding of how it works. One therapist who gives aromatherapy as well as reiki said: "Whenever I see that

I have someone coming to me for reiki treatment in my appointments book, I feel pleased. I appreciate that afterwards I will feel almost as much benefit as the receiver."

To give reiki also heightens the giver's sensitivity, since it gives her a way to "tune in" to someone else's problem, a problem which perhaps the person is unable to express verbally.

Giving thanks

It is traditional to give thanks for reiki after each treatment and after a class. You can do this in any way that feels appropriate, or simply repeat three times: "Thank you for the reiki."

This helps you to remember it is the universal energy, rather than your own energy, that is doing the healing. Remembering to give thanks for reiki is a mark of humility and gratitude.

Positive Cocoon

"I have been held and protected by reiki. Now I have the energy and the attitude to focus and heal myself." A reiki practitioner

REAPING THE
REWARDS

Reiki energy works in many different ways, affecting the receiver on all levels. You may find that it brings you new confidence in your life direction, an easing of physical pain, or improved ways of relating to others. Simply being open to reiki healing can benefit and improve your life immeasurably. As well as receiving treatments, you may also like to enhance your well-being by adopting a healthy lifestyle. Looking after your physical self will calm the mind too, and making space for yoga or meditation can help to improve your outlook.

The Emotional Effects

Allow yourself to feel

A reiki treatment may help many people to release long-held emotional pain.

Reiki treatments generally motivate people and increase their ability to make decisions. They become less fearful if they are prone to feeling anxious. Reiki increases self-confidence and self-esteem. It decreases irritability and impatience and gives the receiver the energy to show tolerance to others. Reiki allows the release of anger and grief, which may often have been held inside for years, even since childhood. The initial effects of a reiki treatment,

whether emotional, spiritual, or physical, may be immediate or manifest themselves between 24 and 36 hours after the treatment.

Helping the release

Reiki healers believe that you cannot separate your emotions from the physical body, even if you make a supreme effort to suppress and ignore your feelings. If emotional issues remain unresolved, there will be energy blockages in the body. These can be cleared with reiki, allowing you to let go of past hurts.

Sometimes, people may feel worse or experience a strong emotional reaction to the reiki treatment. This may take the form of sobbing, hysterical laughter, or overwhelming fatigue.

This can be disturbing for both the receiver and the inexperienced reiki practitioner, who may feel unable to help or unsure what to do. It is best for the receiver to express the emotion, to cry or to laugh, until he feels ready to continue with the session. A calm, comforting presence is often all that is needed. It may also be helpful for the recipient to hear that an emotional release is quite common.

Case History

Karen, 37, suffered a major depressive breakdown and had to take several months off her work as a teacher. She was treated by a psychiatrist and was prescribed anti-depressants. She experienced adverse reactions to them and turned to reiki.

Karen received short, very gentle treatments every few days and was encouraged by her practitioner to talk about her feelings and express whatever she felt able to about her experiences. Gradually Karen began to recover her self-esteem and access a sense of calm. She has been discharged by her doctor and has returned to work.

Life is still not easy for Karen, and she continues to face many challenges in her work. However, she has now completed level 1 reiki, which enables her to have a daily self-treatment and provide support to colleagues. She is no longer taking any medication.

The Open Door

"All my life I have felt as though I have been knocking on doors and no one has answered. But reiki invited me in." A reiki receiver

A NEW CONFIDENCE

Lack or loss of self-esteem is the most common factor that holds us back from realizing our full potential. Many of us lack belief in ourselves and our abilities. We tend to denigrate ourselves for things that we haven't done and fail to congratulate ourselves for what we have achieved in our lives. We may take criticism to heart and feel inadequate. Even when we do perceive achievements, we tend to attribute them to luck or to being in the right place at the right time.

Winning spirit
With regular reiki treatments, you may find yourself able to embrace new challenges.

Focusing on self-belief
Reiki gives people the healing energy they need in order to formulate their goals and realize their full potential.

Feeling no fear
New-found confidence in previously stressful situations is one of reiki's gifts.

The Spiritual Effects

Inner calm
Many of us crave spiritual peace and contentment. This is what reiki offers us.

Reiki is believed by its practitioners and masters to help those who practise it to lead a better life, morally, socially, and spiritually.

The spiritual effects of reiki can be all-embracing, putting people in touch – sometimes for the first time – with their inner life, their spiritual convictions, and their religious beliefs. Spirituality is, of course, a matter of personal choice. Many people believe that one can lead a life of purity or morality without necessarily adhering to formal religious beliefs or attending church, synagogue, or mosque. Many people live their lives contentedly without feeling the need for a belief in a superior being.

Spiritual opening

Reiki practitioners believe that reiki may put some people in touch with God, Allah, or Buddha, according to the individual's faith, and that reiki enhances their existing beliefs.

A spiritual awakening may happen instantly, dramatically, with reiki, or it may take years. Generally, the spiritual effects of reiki are experienced within the first day or two of treatment, although they may take longer.

Practitioners and masters believe that reiki reconnects us with a sense of who we are and our place in the universe. This feeling of connectedness removes a layer of illusion or doubt that prevents us from experiencing fully our potential, both in terms of our own development as a person and in terms of feeling at one with the universe.

The universal life energy that flows through people as they give or receive reiki is a powerful vibrating force that both energizes and harmonizes. Many people report feeling more loving towards themselves after a treatment, and, in turn, towards others.

Case History

Denise, 28, is an artist who has used reiki numerous ways. She has given reiki to friends, to her family, to animals, and, most of all, to herself. On a flight to Miami, she treated a flight attendant for a bad knee. He was able to continue working throughout the long journey. However, she believes that reiki is more than helping a sore knee, or other physical problem, and thinks that it connects her with an inner calmness and strength. Denise works on the conviction that reiki is a friend which will help her in everything she does. Reiki has given Denise an extra insight into the pain and traumas that the people she meets from day to day have to suffer. Since using reiki, she finds that she listens more intently and is more perceptive than before.

A Sense of Belonging

"I know now where I came from and where I am going on life's beautiful journey. I know where I am in the universe." A reiki practitioner

Journey through life
Some people feel reborn when they begin reiki, which sustains them on a new life path.

TRANSFORMING EFFECTS
The effects of reiki can be significant, encouraging people to take a new direction. Some people acquire a new ability to enjoy life through the reduction of pain. Others may benefit by an improved family life, or in their relationships with co-workers. The transformation may take the form of a change from a frenetic lifestyle to one of calm control. Transformation can be subtle, and it may occur over a long period of time, with friends and family barely noticing the positive changes.

Sudden life changes
After having reiki, people may notice opportunities that they had not seen before. Reiki can help to marshal the energy and motivation to take advantage of these openings. Internal changes may be accompanied by physical transformation as the eyes start to sparkle, breathing deepens, and a more positive attitude develops.

A new way
As when a butterfly emerges from a chrysalis, a change of consciousness brought about by reiki can transform life.

Expanding horizons
Reiki can open up the world, giving people the confidence to look further ahead and branch out in new directions.

The Physical Effects

Flush out the toxins
Water is an essential element of health, because it rids the body of toxins and alleviates fatigue.

Reiki is said to have a detoxifying action upon the body. This may mean that you find you need to visit the lavatory more frequently than usual after treatment, you may sweat more, and your stomach may rumble. You may pass wind more frequently. Do not worry about any of these occurrences. They are natural, although they can be a little embarrassing in company. Because of reiki's detoxifying effect, it is important to drink as much

water as you can before and after a treatment. In any case, the minimum that you should drink for optimum health is eight glasses of water a day – and it doesn't count when taken as tea or coffee. Indeed, if you take in caffeine, you will need to drink more than eight glasses of water a day in order to flush out the body's systems and expel the toxins. Guidelines on adopting a healthy and relaxed lifestyle are described on pages 156–73.

Healing response

The physical effects of reiki may be seen after treatment and/or after a reiki class when you receive attunements. Some people find that their pain becomes a little worse before disappearing for good.

Sometimes, the pain simply goes. In other instances, a totally unrelated pain may manifest itself somewhere in the body for a short time before the sufferer is left completely free of pain within a day or two. In short, reiki's healing effect may be felt instantly or may take longer, and it is possible too that you may feel worse before you feel better. For some people, pain that results from a long-term disorder may remain. However, even in these cases healing may help to make the pain more tolerable, increase relaxation, lessen fatigue, and raise energy levels.

Medical symptoms

It is always wise for recipients to check out any symptoms and pains with a doctor before having reiki treatment, or during a course of treatment. Likewise, anyone experiencing a psychiatric condition is advised to consult his doctor before embarking on a course of reiki, and should also inform the reiki practitioner if treatment goes ahead.

Reiki is not intended to be a substitute for any type of medical, hospital, or psychiatric treatment.

From the Heart

"My palpitations have stopped and I have more energy than I had 20 years ago. Life has taken on a golden glow." A reiki receiver

In tune with life
*Even the simplest pleasures can
be enhanced once people
have received the gift of reiki.*

A HEALTHIER BODY
The physical effects of reiki, which may be apparent instantly, or within a day or two of treatment, can include increased energy levels, a physical sense of relaxation, bodily calm, a slower heartbeat, lower blood pressure, and alleviation of aches and pain (including migraine and toothache). Asthma, eczema, and other long-term conditions can also be improved by regular treatments.

From here to eternity
*Chronic fatigue sufferers report
feeling rejuvenated and full of
life following a course of reiki.*

For many years Lynne, a 52-year-old housewife, had been unable to walk for more than five minutes at a time. She took a reiki course in 2000 and feels she has been given a new lease of life. On a recent holiday, she found, to her delight, that she could walk for an hour or more without becoming breathless.

Learning new tricks

Reiki motivates people to take up challenges, and to develop new interests, at any age.

New-found flexibility

Stiffening of the bones and joints – common in old age – can be eased by reiki.

Fit for life

Reiki receivers often enjoy increased energy levels after beginning reiki treatment.

Healthy Eating

Taking the waters
*Let the cleansing power of reiki
wash over the mind, body, and
spirit, and revitalize your system
with an energy-giving diet.*

Adopting a healthy way of life has obvious benefits – enhancing physical health and improving mental and spiritual well-being. It is also possible to attain a deeper awareness of yourself and of other people through following a vitality and relaxation programme.

Eating the right food, having regular mealtimes, and drinking enough water are among the most vital aspects of healthy living. In general, the guidelines on these and the following pages can be followed on a daily basis. However, you should consult your doctor before

making any major changes to your lifestyle, particularly if you have an existing medical condition.

Food for cleansing

Generally, you should try to eat as much fresh food as possible and avoid processed foods as much as you can. You need a varied diet that includes plenty of fresh fruit and vegetables. You also want to make sure that your diet provides a good intake of the main nutrients, such as:

• Protein from meat, poultry, and fish;

• Smaller amounts of protein and calcium from dairy products, such as eggs, cheese, milk, and milk products;

• Protein derived from nuts, peas, lentils, and pulses;

• Carbohydrates and fibre from pulses and grains in the form of barley and bran, for example. Fruit and vegetables also provide fibre and carbohydrates, to a lesser extent.

If you are vegetarian, eat more from groups 2 and 3, and if you are vegan, eat more from group 3. In these cases,

you should take extra care to ensure you are getting enough protein. One way to increase your protein intake is to eat beans and wheat together, as their combined proteins will give you the same amount of protein as meat.

Eat one of the following at least once a day for optimum cleansing and detoxification: wholewheat cereal, wholemeal bread, wholemeal pasta, or wholemeal savoury biscuits without added sugar. Have as much salad and vegetables as you can manage.

Healing power of water

Starting the day with a glass of water with a squeeze of fresh lemon juice helps to cleanse the system. You should also drink at least eight glasses of water every day, and make sure that you drink at least one glass of water before and after a reiki treatment.

Fuelling the Body

Caring for your body, and providing it with a good diet, is a simple way of showing respect for yourself and your physical health.

Invigorate yourself
Boost your energy levels, and banish fatigue with at least eight glasses of water a day.

FOOD FOR FITNESS

Improving your diet and increasing your intake of water helps you to feel better physically, mentally, and spiritually. Caring for the body is a vital step in increasing your energy levels. Many people turn to junk food when they are depressed, but it offers little nutrition and creates an extra burden of toxins for the body to eliminate.

Sweet delights
Include plenty of fruit in your diet. Coconut is a good source of fibre, and avocado is rich in potassium and vitamin E.

Nature's medicine
Garlic may help to lower blood pressure, acts as a nasal decongestant, and has anti-viral and antibacterial properties.

Dump the junk
We may gratify ourselves orally, by having treats such as chocolate and cigarettes, to compensate for failures, shortcomings, and disappointments. You may find it easier to give these up when you start treating yourself with regular reiki.

158

Balancing foods
A vegetarian diet is increasingly popular, but include plenty of nuts and pulses to increase your protein intake.

Liquid Goodness

You can pulp or liquidize almost any fruit or vegetable, which is an excellent way to increase your vitamin intake. Try these combinations:

- banana and kiwi
- lemon and banana
- carrot and apple
- cucumber and celery
- radish and cucumber

Your Vitality Programme

Sweet dreams
Reiki helps us to overcome problems and sleep well, an essential for good health.

Adopting a programme for vitality comprises several elements: following a healthy diet and drinking plenty of water (see previous pages), exercise, sleep, and dry skin brushing. You may also like to fast for one day each week or month. Don't forget to include a daily reiki self-treatment (see pages 138–39) since reiki promotes the elimination of toxins and assists good, deep sleep.

Introducing all these elements into your life, even if it is just for a week or two, will reap benefits. When you begin a vitality programme, particularly if it involves a major change from your current lifestyle, choose a period in your year when you will not have a great many social or work demands. You should also check with your doctor.

Exercise and sleep

Choose a form of exercise that suits you, and try to exercise in the fresh air when possible. You should exercise for at least 20 minutes three times a week. Introducing yoga, meditation, or relaxation exercises into your life can help to calm the mind and alleviate stress (see following pages).

Try to go to bed at the same time each night, and let yourself sleep for roughly the same number of hours. A short self-reiki can greatly enhance your sleep (see pages 132–33).

Skin brushing

Brush your skin briskly with a bristle brush for five minutes before bathing, using long, upward movements over the whole body, towards the heart. Skin

brushing stimulates the circulation and
rejuvenates the nervous system because
of the hundreds of nerve endings in the
skin. It also removes dead skin layers
and other impurities, keeping the pores
open and unclogged, and increases the
elimination capacity of the skin. It is
important that your skin brush be yours
alone, so do not lend it to other people.

Detox guidelines

When you first start on cleansing and
revitalizing your system, your skin may
erupt as toxins are expelled from your
body. Soon, your skin will become
clear and your eyes brighter.

Rapid detox is achieved through
eating only one fruit or only one
vegetable for one or two consecutive
days, remembering of course to drink at
least eight glasses of water a day. Fast
only under medical supervision.

Quality of Life

A healthy life is the easy life. With good
sleep, good food, good activity, and plenty of
water, your energy levels will rise.

Calming yourself
Before you start the relaxation exercises, be sure first to spend five minutes breathing calmly.

RELAXATION EXERCISES

Most people underbreathe or breathe too shallowly, breathing from the chest area or even just the throat. You should breathe from the abdomen and the diaphragm. If you watch a baby or a young child breathe, you will see that he does this naturally. His tummy rises as he breathes in, and it falls as he breathes out. It is only later in life that we acquire poor, rushed, anxious breathing habits.

Learning to breathe
Singers are taught to breathe as children do, from the abdomen. Breathing from your abdomen can induce a feeling of calm and relaxation and can be an excellent way to regain perspective during a stressful day. Simply stand with shoulders relaxed and feel your breath slowly coming up from the abdomen. At the same time feel the diaphragm and rib cage expanding. Hold the breath for a moment and then let it go very gradually.

Begin with the feet, letting them roll out to the sides as they relax

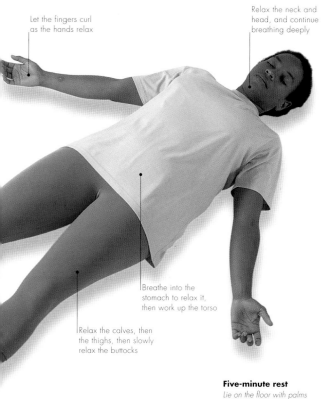

Let the fingers curl
as the hands relax

Relax the neck and
head, and continue
breathing deeply

Breathe into the
stomach to relax it,
then work up the torso

Relax the calves, then
the thighs, then slowly
relax the buttocks

Five-minute rest

*Lie on the floor with palms
upwards and your arms
outstretched. Relax the body,
working upwards from the feet.
Lie still for a few minutes before
getting up slowly.*

How Reiki Enhances Other Therapies

Enhancing the effects
Give reiki to your oils and herbal essences. This will imbue them with energy and increase their healing effects.

Using reiki does not mean you cannot benefit from other complementary therapies, particularly if you are already finding them helpful. Many therapists use reiki to increase the holistic nature of their therapies. Reiki can also be used to protect against the negative side effects of the treatments used in conventional medical practice: reiki helps to relax and prepare people for surgery, for example. In brief, reiki can improve the effectiveness of both herbal medicines and orthodox drugs.

You can give yourself reiki before treatment begins, to enhance its effect. If you intend giving yourself reiki before going for another form of treatment, it is only courteous to inform the practitioner of what you are doing.

Reiki can provide the therapist or practitioner of another therapy with additional stamina, strength, and patience to help and support him while he is treating his patients.

Aromatherapy and massage

Giving reiki to aromatherapy oils before they are used is said to help infuse them with healing energy. Herbal or flower remedies may also be given reiki to enhance their effects.

In massage or shiatsu, areas of tension can be given reiki. Similarly some osteopaths or chiropractors may give reiki to troubled areas.

Crystal healing

Crystals are believed to enhance
and focus energy, which can then be
directed to specific sites of energy
blockage. Reiki is sometimes used at
the start of a crystal-healing treatment to
correct the root cause of the disorder.

Hypnotherapy

Using the first five positions of reiki prior
to hypnosis can shorten the time that it
takes for someone to become
hypnotized. There are similarities
between the deeply relaxed state of
hypnotherapy and reiki.

Similarly, meditation practice,
chanting, and singing may all benefit
from being combined with reiki. The
relaxing effects of reiki help to release
tension and deepen the breathing.

Compatibility

Reiki has the ability to blend with and enhance
the power and the energy of all the other
therapies; it also makes meditation deeper.

Loosen up
Flick out the hands to release tension. This also benefits the shoulders, arms, and neck.

SPECIALIZED STRETCHES
Certain practices, such as yoga, tai chi, or chi kung, work to improve energy flow through the system. They therefore work extremely well with regular reiki treatments. However, if you do not have time to integrate one of the practices into your day, try these quick stretches to improve your overall energy flow.

Arm swings
1 Stand easy, feet apart, slight flex in knees. Cross your hands in front of you. Breathe in.

2 Breathe out as you swing your arms down and away from you. Cross in front of you again and repeat twice more.

3 Breathe in and swing your arms up over your head. Breathe out as you swing them down. Repeat three times.

Keep the palm facing forwards

Circle the arm back

Side stretches

Stand upright, with your shoulders relaxed and chin up. Slowly bend to the right, sliding the hand down the leg. Stretch the left side of the neck, waist, and upper body. Hold for a few moments. Slowly return to a standing position and pause for a rest. Repeat the routine on the other side. Then repeat the entire routine several times.

Gently stretch the neck

Slide the left hand down the leg

Shoulder circles

Raise the arm above the head, gently swinging backwards. Repeat with the other arm.

Meditation

Winding down
As the breath comes in say a silent "re", and as it goes out say a silent "lax". Do this for about ten minutes.

The effects of meditation are primarily centring and calming. The practice of reiki is itself almost a form of meditation, with which it shares many similarities.

Introducing meditation into your life can calm the mind, soothe the body, and refresh the spirit. Even a five-minute session each morning can help you start the day in a relaxed frame of mind. Many people say that once they have been attuned for reiki, they achieve a

deeper, more relaxed state in their meditation practice with much less conscious effort. The quiet time of a reiki treatment session may seem less strange for the giver or the receiver if he is familiar with meditation.

Your focus

To meditate, you may choose to focus on a single object in front of you, such as a lighted candle or a flower, or to focus on the inhalation and exhalation of your breath, It is best to choose one focus, and remain with that for however long you have decided to meditate. Many people find it helpful to set an alarm, so that they can concentrate on their practice rather than worrying about how much time has passed.

Removing energy blocks

Using meditation in a reiki session may help to break down energy blockages. Closing your eyes and focusing on particular areas while you are giving or receiving a treatment helps to marshal the universal energy and channel it to the places where it is most needed. You may find that certain areas of the body are drawing little energy compared with others. Sometimes the practitioner or receiver feels warmth in the hands or in a particular area – signifying a lot of energy being drawn into the receiver. Equally, either may feel a tingling somewhere, or nothing at all.

If you sense any blockages, imagine yourself grasping the blocked energy and pulling it up and out of your own body. This will help to free the blocked area, and allow the energy to flow smoothly once again.

Clearing the mind

Before meditation, try this simple practice to rid yourself of unwanted thoughts. Simply allow words in the mind to emerge as sounds, while gently shaking your head and hands.

Tranquillity

Try this affirmation before meditating: "I am quiet and all around me is quiet. Tranquillity is mine to give and mine to receive."

Energy from all around
Draw in energy from the atmosphere by visualizing the literal meaning of reiki: life force.

VISUALIZATION
You can use visualization techniques in a number of different ways. You may spend time visualizing a beautiful scene in order to reduce your anxiety level and establish a calm feeling within. Or you can visualize a part of your body that is in pain bathed in a healing golden light. There are many ways to use this practice. One of the most valuable is to use visualization as a sleeping aid by imagining a tranquil scene.

Travels in your mind
You can visualize a situation that you are striving towards by manifesting a positive picture and holding that picture in your mind. You can use this technique to invoke a calm scene at a chaotic time of your life or to fight disease by imagining that the part of you that is ill has recovered, for example. For general well-being, you may also like to focus on the reiki symbols or visualize a person who is a source of inspiration to you.

The essence of beauty
Sit quietly for ten minutes with the image of a flower in your mind. Look closely at each petal.

Hope on the horizon
The image of a magnificent sunset soothes a troubled mind. Look at all the different colours.

Just close your eyes
Ease feelings of anger or frustration by picturing a tropical, sun-drenched beach.

Affirmations

Affirming your strength
*Repeat your chosen affirmations
in front of a mirror every day
to reinforce their potency.*

Using affirmations helps you to
decide and be clear about what
you really want. Repeating these
affirmations is thought to help you
achieve your desired path, because
they can strengthen motivation, direct
your energies, and help to reinforce
decisions you have taken.

Affirmations can be used both for the
self and for others. You can think of
some of the relevant affirmations that
you have chosen, for example, when
you are receiving a reiki treatment.

These are some of the positive
affirmations that you might like to use:
- I am well.
- I am whole and safe.
- Let light and love flow over and
through me/you.

Some practitioners view affirmations
as a verbal variation on visualization
techniques. Rather than seeing your
desired situation as a picture, you
describe it in short phrases and repeat
them to yourself at least once a day,
and ideally at least three times a day.

The repeat-and-reinforcement
technique is a valuable tool of positive-
thinking therapies – and many people
believe that it works. All you have to do
is practise. As one practitioner has
described it, you already hold the
cards, all you have to do is play them.

Choosing your affirmations

First, decide upon your desired goals,
and then devise a simple affirmation for
each particular goal that will mean
something to you personally. Your
goals could include:

- Being kind to others;
- Looking after your parents;
- Giving up smoking;
- Paying more attention to your work;
- Being nicer to your children;
- Making more time for your family;
- Improving self-confidence;
- Banishing ill heath in others;
- Banishing unhappiness in others.

Improving self-confidence

If you were to select this as a goal, you might devise affirmations such as these:

- I am a kind person;
- I am an attractive person (pinpoint your attractive personal qualities and physical features);
- I have friends;
- My family loves me.

All these affirmations, repeated daily in front of a mirror, would help to improve your self-confidence.

Just For Today...

For one day, do not get angry, do not worry, earn your living honestly, honour your elders, and show gratitude to every living thing.

PROGRESSING WITH REIKI

As your understanding of reiki deepens and strengthens, and it becomes more central to your way of living, you may feel that you want to continue learning. Reiki 1 opens up the body to the energy of reiki, and you will need some time to assimilate and make the most of the effects. This period is a vital preparation for the higher levels, which work on opening up the mental, emotional, and spiritual planes of your being. ✎ Developing your understanding of reiki is a journey and a progression that is best undertaken over months or years, particularly if you want to train to be a reiki master.

Moving from First to Second Level

Reach for the stars
Once you have absorbed reiki 1, you may want to move onwards and upwards.

Once you have received the first four attunements and have developed an understanding of the first level of reiki, you will be able to progress to a higher level. However, you should practise reiki regularly for at least three months before moving from level 1 to level 2. Many masters believe it is better if you can spend six months developing your understanding of this stage of the reiki journey, particularly if you are thinking of eventually practising reiki as a therapist, which requires a deep awareness of the healing.

How you assimilate and use what you have learned is up to you. Most reiki masters recommend that you treat yourself daily with reiki. Giving yourself a short treatment in the morning, to energize your day, and another at night, to help ensure a good night's sleep, is an excellent way of bringing reiki into your everyday life.

It is also worth setting aside the time to give yourself a full treatment once a week, or more often if you can manage it. Practising regularly on friends and relatives, and even family pets, will also help you to strengthen your understanding of reiki and enhance the flow of energy, as well as benefiting those around you.

Generally, the longer the period over which you have practised level 1, the more opportunity you have to broaden the scope of uses when you study level 2. Spending sufficient time on developing the basic techniques of reiki will also help to ensure that you are fully ready to further your understanding of the power of reiki, the universe, and the self in level 2.

A personal choice

There is nothing to say that you have to move on from level 1 to level 2, or, again, from level 2 onwards. Many people are happy to learn and use reiki healing at the first level, but do not wish to take their learning any further.

Moving on from one level to the next is a personal decision that requires considerable commitment to yourself and to reiki. Only you know if you want to make it and if reiki is the right way forwards for you.

Trust in Everyday Things

Trust the reiki and you will learn to trust yourself. Use it every day so that your understanding continues to grow.

Stronger flow
Many people notice increased heat in their hands when they treat after studying level 2.

DEEPER HEALING
The level 2 attunement intensifies the energy vibrations and helps to open you up to a higher level of consciousness. Studying second degree means working on the mental and emotional levels of being. As we continue to heal ourselves, we deepen our ability to heal others. Level 2 enables students to extend reiki healing to people who are not available for hands-on healing because of physical distance.

Doves of peace
Gliding freely in the sky, the wings of the doves express the strength and direction of reiki.

Looking outwards

Level 2 helps you to expand
your horizons and extend
your healing energy to people
all over the world, as well as
to situations, relationships, life
events (such as operations,
interviews, or driving tests),
and even places.

Going deeper

*You may notice a greater depth
to your healing after taking the
second degree.*

Keeping close

*Using distant-healing techniques
may help you to keep a
connection with a loved one
even when you are separated.*

Distant Healing

Embracing the planet
There is a limitless scope to distant healing. You can send it to the whole world.

Sending distant healing is a powerful way of helping people when you cannot give them hands-on healing. However, as with any reiki treatment, you should ask the receiver's permission before sending them healing. You may want to use a photograph or your own body for proxy positions, to send the equivalent of a full treatment. The latter is often better, in that you may receive energetic feedback, which will assist you with the treatment. A more simple method is to simply focus on a person and hold them in your mind for a few minutes, visualizing the (level 2) sacred reiki symbols and repeating the mantras (see page 72). You can also use this method to send reiki to situations or places.

To reiki negative issues or specific problems, you may like to make a written note of the problem on a piece of paper. Sit and focus on it for few moments, again using the symbols and mantras. Then place the paper in a metal or other fireproof dish, and set it alight. As it burns, focus on bringing positive healing to the situation.

Power of the group

Sending distant reiki with a group of reiki practitioners amplifies the effect. If the group is in the same place, you may like to sit in a circle, holding your hands up with palms turned outwards. Make sure that everyone knows the full name of the person or situation to which you are sending reiki. Alternatively, you can place a photograph or object representing the person or situation to be healed in the centre of the group. Say the person's name and name her situation. Each one in the group focuses on the recipient for a few minutes, in silence. A nurturing way to end a session and benefit from group energy can be for all the givers to finish by sending healing to themselves.

Sharing groups

Many second-degree students set up reiki-sharing groups specifically to send distant healing to those in need. If members cannot come together, the group may use a "telephone tree", where each member of the group passes on requests for help or support to one or two other members. Each member sends distant healing to the agreed recipient, either at a pre-arranged time, or at her convenience.

Heart Connection

Absence is said to make the heart fonder. Distant healing is a way of bringing people close, even when they are physically apart.

The universal language
*Reiki uses the language of
touch, instinct, and energy,
known all over the world.*

EXTENDING BOUNDARIES Learning
distant healing can open up physical or mental boundaries, allowing you to
help where before you might not have felt able to do so, or where distance
kept you apart from someone. Because level 2 works on the mental and
emotional levels, it offers an opportunity to loosen mental blocks, and improve
your ability to communicate. Group work is a vital part of this process.

A list for healing
If there are several people to
whom you want to send
distant healing, some masters
recommend listing their names
on a piece of paper. You can
then focus on the list to send
healing to everyone on it.
Some people keep the list in
a box charged with reiki
energy to increase the effect.

A reiki list saves you
time if you are
sending healing to
more than one person

Hold your attention on the receiver for ten minutes

Alone or with others

Level 2 develops your healing skills and also shows you how to work with other people to send healing. A group can engage in distant healing, or hands-on treatment, whichever is most appropriate. In both cases, the healing process can be strengthened.

Create a calm, safe space for the group

Group Treatments

Added spiritual power

Friends who are all practitioners often find a tremendous spiritual charge through group reiki.

As you gain in experience and depth, you can work with other reiki practitioners to give hands-on group healing. The techniques for working with more than one giver are taught in level 2 classes, with groups of students working on a single recipient.

Theoretically, any number of people can give hands-on healing to a single participant, but it generally works best if you use between 2 and 20 givers. Using more than one giver speeds up treatment and seems to amplify and deepen the effect, often giving a more intense experience. Some masters say that the strength of the healing is multiplied by the number of givers, so that receiving a 10-minute treatment from four people is equivalent to having a 40-minute healing session from a single practitioner.

A group giving

With a large group of givers, each person can focus on a single area for the length of the session; with only a few givers, you will have to move around the body during the session. It is best to arrange beforehand which areas each person will cover and to agree a signal so that you all change areas at the same time.

Take a few minutes before beginning the treatment, to make sure all the participants are comfortable. Some people like to share a short meditation to help centre the group and its energy. However, this is not always necessary, as the healing has a calming effect.

The giver receives

Often, practitioners do a lot of giving to friends and family, particularly when they start practising. Receiving from a group of like-minded people can yield a powerful sense of comfort and healing. Many reiki adherents enjoy exchanging treatments in this way and find that participating in a group is a reassuring way of using reiki energy.

Case History

Sandi Leir Shuffrey is a well-respected reiki master, who has been practising and teaching for more than a decade. She once held a review class for 17 students, 8 of whom had also taken the second degree of reiki. It was Midsummer's Day, with scorching hot sunshine when Sandi lay on a bench in the garden to receive a group healing. Thirty-four hands were laid on her. Sandi says that she felt as if she had "died and gone to heaven". The "hands-on" experience felt like a world embrace that healed all her childhood pain, loneliness, and anger at once.

Tradition of Exchange

Everyone benefits from a group healing session – the recipient and all the givers, who share a powerful experience.

AWARENESS OF CHANGE

It is useful to monitor your energy levels in order to chart your progress in reiki. The best way of ensuring your awareness of change is to keep a journal. This will help you to notice gradual changes, as well as any major life events. Take note of other people's responses to you and see how they differ from the responses you commonly met before you started learning reiki. Many reiki adherents say that other people have become noticeably more positive towards them.

Metamorphosis
As your new outlook and attitudes start to take shape, you may experience changes.

Recording your feelings
You can more easily monitor the changes brought about by reiki if you keep a journal or log.

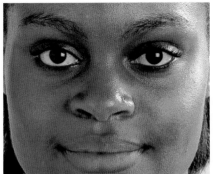

The windows of the soul
Your friends may perceive the changes in you through a more serene expression in your eyes.

Bathed in beauty
You may notice an ease in your meditation practice when you start to progress in reiki.

Your Relationship with Your Master

Deeper awareness
Your relationship and your talks with your reiki master are an all-important part of your training.

Talking to your reiki master is an important element in the process of deepening your spiritual awareness and appraising your journey of exploration. This can be useful for people at all stages of reiki, but many people feel that they particularly need a close relationship with their master when they begin to explore reiki at the second and higher levels.

It can be of inestimable value to discuss any doubts and questions that you may have, and most masters will be happy to support you in this process. This will help to build your confidence and resolve any anxieties that you may have. Informal chats with your master can be invaluable in reducing confusion and providing you with reassurance and affirmation of your chosen life path when you need it.

Do not hesitate to raise any questions or doubts that you may have with your master. Listening to students is an important part the master's role. She has assumed responsibility for helping you progress and is well aware that her students may often need to talk about their experiences.

Witnessing your progress
A master may be able to help you to review your life periodically and to look at what has changed in the months since your last discussion. The effects

of reiki may be gradual and may not be noticed straightaway by the student. The master may be in a better situation to see these shifts and feed back your progress to you.

You may not have noticed that you are getting on better with your boss, for example, or are enjoying time with your children more. It is often helpful to see someone who can remind you to stop for a moment and think back to how you were before you started reiki.

A reiki master may help you to assess the different areas of your life and how you are coping with any difficulties that may arise. Talking to your master when you feel the need is a vital part of making the decision to learn reiki at the higher levels, if that is what you would like to do in the future.

Hearing Your Master

Spending time with your master helps to unlock the teachings and reveal a new universe inside and around us.

The element of life
The strands of consciousness weave together to form an unbreakable chain of spirituality.

MOVING ON TO MASTERSHIP The

master levels of reiki are not for everyone, and they can be difficult and challenging. Taking this route requires a lifelong commitment, considerable self-development, and the regular use of reiki, as both giver and receiver. Because taking the master levels of reiki constitutes such an important step, it merits careful consideration and discussion with your master.

Spiritual dynamic
An ever-deepening reservoir of awareness through using reiki is apparent in mind and body.

When you are ready
You may gradually become aware of a strengthening and deepening of spiritual consciousness and an overwhelming sense that you are getting in touch with the universal energy at a deep level. This may be a sign that you are ready to move on to the higher levels of reiki.

Becoming a Master

Humility and sensitivity
If you are destined to become a master, you may be invited to take the training.

As you develop an understanding of level 2 and practise the techniques, you may feel a greater pull to progress and embrace reiki more fully. Levels 3 and 4 (the master levels) work on the emotional and spiritual levels of being, opening students up to a deeper connection with the life-force energy.

The reiki master uses reiki energy in the same way as other students, but has simply travelled further along the reiki path. This road may prove challenging,

frightening, and joyous all at once. As you start to open to the higher levels, you may find that every step you take enhances the balance of energy and accelerates the flow of reiki.

Reiki chooses you

Traditionally, one was invited to become a master by an existing master. Many people say that reiki chooses its masters, rather than individuals making the decision for themselves. Most existing masters will say that they felt a deep inner conviction that reiki was the right path for them.

Ideally, you should have used reiki for at least two years before embarking on the master levels. Training for mastership may take between several months and several years. You may decide simply to concentrate on your own development, in level 3, but not to take on the responsibility of teaching others, which would take you to level 4.

If you decide to take level 4 and become a teaching master, you will need to consider practical issues such as finding premises where you can teach classes. You may also like to contact one of the reiki organizations listed at the end of the book.

Case History

Paul, aged 40, is a doctor who suffered for five years with ME (chronic fatigue syndrome). He turned to reiki to help him cope with the symptoms, and he has had a long and positive journey through the reiki levels.

At first Paul was sceptical about reiki because he had been trained in Western medicine. However, his ME was not responding to treatment, and a friend offered him reiki. Finding it extremely helpful, Paul decided to learn the techniques. Since then, he has progressed to level 2, and on to level 3. When he first considered doing level 3, Paul felt a strong instinct that he should do it and he is now reaping the rewards. Paul feels that his mind and body have come into harmony, and his awareness is growing stronger. Reiki has given Paul a freedom to be himself and he feels he has the confidence to follow his own path, whether or not others think it right.

Your Place in the World

Becoming a master may help you to come to a point of acceptance and enjoyment of the universe and your place within it.

Petals unfolding
*Many therapists are richly
rewarded by seeing their
patients blossom after reiki.*

BECOMING A THERAPIST

In reiki, everyone is her own therapist, but there are times when people need the help of a professional. If you are considering becoming a reiki therapist, you need to ensure that you have sufficient depth of experience. It is also part of caring to consider the safety and comfort of your clients. Further guidelines for what you need to become a therapist are listed on the following pages.

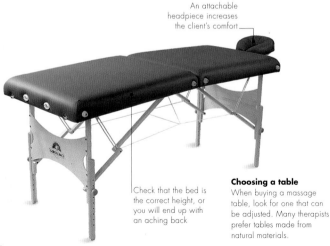

An attachable
headpiece increases
the client's comfort

Check that the bed is
the correct height, or
you will end up with
an aching back

Choosing a table
When buying a massage
table, look for one that can
be adjusted. Many therapists
prefer tables made from
natural materials.

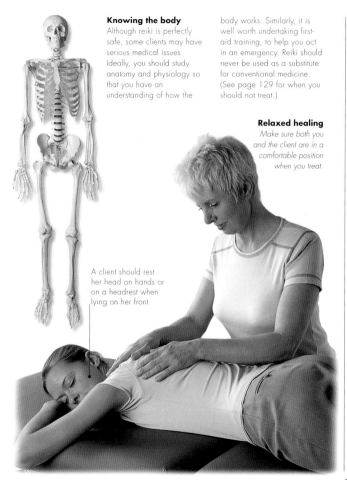

Knowing the body

Although reiki is perfectly safe, some clients may have serious medical issues. Ideally, you should study anatomy and physiology so that you have an understanding of how the body works. Similarly, it is well worth undertaking first-aid training, to help you act in an emergency. Reiki should never be used as a substitute for conventional medicine. (See page 129 for when you should not treat.)

Relaxed healing

Make sure both you and the client are in a comfortable position when you treat.

A client should rest her head on hands or on a headrest when lying on her front

What a Therapist Needs

Gift of giving
*It is important to be punctual,
calm, and steady before you
give a reiki treatment.*

There are no specific requirements for
becoming a reiki therapist. However,
the following guidelines will help to
ensure that you are ready to treat.

Experience of reiki

Before you consider becoming a reiki
therapist, you need to have completed
the first degree and to have practised
the techniques for at least three months,
but preferably six or more. This means
treating yourself daily and giving reiki to
a variety of other people (see Giving a
Treatment, pages 90–141).

It is vital that you complete second
degree and practise distant and hands-
on healing for several months, even if
you are already a professional
practitioner in another therapy. This
deepens your understanding and shows
that you have demonstrated the
necessary commitment to reiki. You
need enough knowledge to support
others and deal with emotional issues
that may arise. It is also helpful to have
an understanding of how the body
works (see pages 194–95).

Anyone can practise reiki after
completing level 1. However, this
does not give you the
necessary skills and understanding to
help others through their healing
processes. If you want to become a
professional reiki therapist and charge
for your services, you will need to
address various practical issues
concerned with setting up a practice
and ensure that your experience and
knowledge of reiki are sufficient.

You should keep a journal of your progress and experiences (see pages 186–87), as well as case histories of the people you treat. You can then discuss these with your master, whose approval you should seek before starting to practise. Ideally, all reiki therapists should also belong to a professional reiki organization.

Professional practice

By law, anyone seeing clients needs professional insurance, both public liability and malpractice. This provides protection for the therapist and the clients. You also need a place to practise that is comfortable, welcoming, and suitable for the purpose (see pages 94–97). Little equipment is needed, but professional reiki therapists should invest in a good, comfortable practice couch (see previous pages).

The Therapist's Role

Remember that the reiki does the healing, not the giver. The therapist provides space and support for the healing to take place.

THE SCOPE OF REIKI

Accessing healing energy can have a direct and positive effect on your health, your relationships, and your life direction. You can use reiki to ease your individual circumstances, or offer it to others, to enhance the lives of family, friends, colleagues, and those you come into contact with. ✍ Distant healing widens the scope of reiki still further, enabling you to reach even those who are living in another country and to bring healing energy to situations and places. You can even use it as part of a movement towards world peace.

A Daily Support

An aura of serenity
*Reiki becomes an integral part
of your being, your motivation,
and your attitudes to everything
and everyone around you.*

Some reiki adherents say that reiki
is like a friend. Because the
energy works through you, it
becomes a part of you and is always
there. You can access reiki energy at
any point of the day, so it can be used
as a constant support. Many people
find simply knowing this gives them the
confidence to look inwards. This can
help to pinpoint and clear old thoughts
and behaviour patterns which may be
holding them back from progressing.

Changing perspective
Using reiki may not take away
problems or solve major life issues.
However, most people find that it
changes the way they see and handle
difficulties. It is easy to become
overwhelmed by a problem and unable
to see the obvious first step towards
resolving it. Giving and receiving reiki
helps to bring you to a place of
calmness. Accessing some mental
space enables you to think more clearly
and therefore recognize whether or not
you are heading in the right direction,
in work, relationships, health, or other
areas of your life.

Shaping your destiny
You may find it revealing to keep a
journal from the time that you start reiki.
Make a note of situations in your
personal, family, and working lives. Set
out the goals you wish to achieve, and
give yourself some kind of time frame in
which to accomplish them. You could
also record your mood and state of
well-being, or otherwise, so that in the

months and years to come, you have a detailed picture of how you were, how you felt, and what you did. This will provide a point of reference between past and present and may help you to see your progress more clearly.

Case History

Hugo, 29, a business journalist, studied level 1 four years ago. He uses it regularly on himself and occasionally treats other people.

Hugo enjoyed his reiki course and has received huge benefits from it. Once he suffered badly from stress and insomnia, and found that he was often arguing with his wife. Now Hugo gives himself reiki when he goes to bed, to help him drop off, and again if he wakes up feeling anxious in the middle of the night. If he has a big deadline coming up, he sometimes asks friends who have studied level 2 to send him distant healing. Using reiki in his day-to-day life has made Hugo feel calmer, and he handles stress better. He feels this has helped his relationship with his wife enormously, and they are just about to celebrate their fifth wedding anniversary.

Belief Creates Reality

"Your beliefs help to shape your reality, and so positive thinking and reiki can help to change the way you live." A reiki master

Time is on your side
You have the time to do whatever it is that you want to do. Start now... and enjoy.

DECIDE YOUR GOALS Determining realistic
goals can help you to make the most of your life and to make it a positive experience. It is important to have some kind of structure in mind for your continuing development. There are some things in life that we must accept as they are, as best we can, for they are unchangeable. For certain goals, however, we need to set targets and take steps to meet them.

Taking charge
Do you ever find yourself saying, "I've always wanted to do that"? Whether it is learning to sing, walking from one end of the country to the other, or working with children, there is nothing stopping you. Take the first step today and get the information you need, then act on it. You can probably achieve more than you think. Look how many people change careers in mid life.

You can do it
It's never too late to learn a new skill. Overcoming any fear of failure is the first step.

FAMILY

CAREER

ROMANCE

ADVENTURE

Bringing Reiki into Daily Life

Using your time well
Try to spend delays in reflection and contemplation, rather than in frustration and irritation.

What most of us need more than anything is more time – or the ability to use the time that we have to the best effect.

Time and motion

One of the chief factors in not having enough time is the fact that many of us are working under pressure. This can make us less productive than we would otherwise be. Reiki can give us clarity, which helps us to resolve tensions, to set priorities, and to work more effectively, with time set aside for relaxation.

Relieving the pressures

Ask yourself if all the things that you do are really necessary. Are there some things that could simply be eliminated from your daily life? Jotting down your daily routine may help you to see where you are wasting time and energy.

Ask yourself if you are taking care of your health. Are you eating and sleeping regularly and well? What are the steps that you need to take in order to improve the ways in which you cope with the everyday pressures? Something quite small, such as taking a walk at lunchtime, may be the key to improving well-being. (See Reaping the Rewards, pages 142–73.)

Give yourself a quick reiki treatment to relieve immediate pressures – before a long journey or a meeting at work, for example. Alternatively you can send distant reiki to your work or to particular situations that you find difficult. Sending distant reiki may enable you to see the source of stress objectively, which can help you to deal with it more effectively and with less emotional involvement.

Balance

It is helpful to start each day with a short reiki treatment, if you can. Many people also use reiki to unwind at night. Reiki helps to impart a sense of belonging to the universe, which can be invaluable. Use this and the clarity you get from regular reiki to scrutinize the three main areas of your life – usually family, home, and work. Try to determine whether or not you have the balance between each that you want.

The Highest Aim

Always aim for the highest goal achievable, for if you only aim for the next step, only the next step will become yours.

Mind and body
The brain interacts with mind and body with a complexity and speed hard even to imagine.

MIND, BODY, AND SPIRIT

Disease can be caused by dis-ease in the mind. If we are anxious, tired, or fearful for too long, for example, and we fail to rest, nourish, and care for ourselves, or if we are lonely or under pressure for too long, eventually the physical body may react. This is one of the reasons why it is important to take stock of your life from time to time. Is it flowing in the way you would like?

Creating your reality
It is now generally accepted that physical illness can be a manifestation of mental or emotional turmoil. Reiki works to soothe the fire of physical disorders by bringing peace and harmony to the mind and spirit. Even chronic illnesses can be helped by reiki, because it goes to the very root of the problem.

Treating the cause

Some practitioners report treating patients with physical defects, such as a stoop, and seeing an improvement after only a few sessions. Even seemingly permanent conditions may be related to emotional or spiritual pain and may be released by reiki.

Spiritual clarity

The landscape of the mind becomes a clear and beautiful picture as reiki does its work.

Case History

Lindsey, 31, a teacher, used to suffer from headaches that lasted for a week at a time. She took a course in reiki in 1999 and felt that it was the most cleansing and spiritually awakening event of her life. Lindsey feels deep gratitude to whatever guided her to attend the first lecture. She describes the feeling that she receives from working on herself as one of deep peace. Lindsey has coupled reiki with personal-growth work and finds that reiki helps to restore and complete her, physically, emotionally, and spiritually.

Helping Your Friends and Family

Reiki knows no crisis
*Invoke reiki to help your family
and friends through any
uncomfortable situations.*

Y ou should always ask permission before giving somebody reiki. However, with family and close friends, you may like to give reiki informally. Giving someone a hug, adding reiki energy, can be a loving, gentle way to offer support. Offer reiki to soothe the discomfort of minor injuries, such as a scraped knee or a cut finger. Children may like to have a reiki treatment before an exam, or you can send distant reiki to help them through. Distant reiki is also useful if older children are away – for example backpacking abroad on a gap year. Some parents worry about their children when they are out at night. Sending reiki to them is a constructive way to set your mind at rest.

Beginnings and endings

Reiki can be invaluable during labour to assist the mother in relaxation and deep breathing. You can give yourself reiki during labour, or a partner or friend can give it, to support you.

A reiki treatment can be comforting to someone who has been bereaved. Not only are adults distraught when they lose a loved one, but children may be inconsolable and less able to express their grief. All will benefit greatly from loving reiki.

Many people feel strongly about their pets. Send reiki to a pet that is ill, or, if it dies, send reiki to comfort the owner.

Case History

Shadow is a 15-year-old German Shepherd who belongs to Marie, a reiki practitioner. The dog was having problems with her back legs because of arthritis. She was panting a lot, seemed to be in discomfort, and was also starting to develop cataracts in her eyes.

When Marie started to give Shadow reiki, the dog relaxed, closed her eyes, and let Marie continue. Marie gave Shadow a couple of treatments lasting 15 to 20 minutes and thought no more about it. The following day Shadow followed Marie around the house, brushing up against her until she gave her more reiki. For the next few days, Marie gave the dog daily treatments. Both Marie and her husband, Mick, noticed a change in Shadow from that time; she was much calmer and the cataracts in her eyes had disappeared. Shadow now receives reiki regularly, and is contented and well.

Marie and Mick know that she does not have long to live, but they feel happy that she can see her last days out in comfort.

To Have and to Hold

If your children are going away, give them a memento to carry with them on their journey, but first charge it with loving reiki energy.

Charged with energy

Place your hands around a pot to encourage plant growth, or give reiki to an injured stem.

REIKI IN YOUR HOME

There are all sorts of ways that you can use reiki in your home. You may like to give your pets a daily treatment and to reiki your house plants, the plants in your garden, and, perhaps, new seeds and cuttings that you have planted. Many people give distant healing to different rooms in the house to help the energy flow.

Troubleshooting

You may wish to use reiki to help you find lost possessions, to loosen a jar that will not open, or even to encourage a car that won't start on a cold morning. You can also reiki your food before you serve it, or in restaurants, particularly if you feel uneasy about how the food has been prepared, or use the techniques to cleanse a room after a family argument.

Animal loving

Many animals respond well to reiki, and a treatment can help you feel even closer to your pet.

Good vibrations

Help every meal to enrich you spiritually as well as physically by giving your food reiki.

Extra special gifts

If you are offering a special gift or keepsake to a loved one, treat it with reiki first.

Plant care

Carry reiki awareness with you as you tend to household plants, sending them love and energy.

Flooding with love

Give reiki to the rooms in your home where you want to keep the energy flowing, and to fill a room's atmosphere with positive, loving vibrations.

Reiki in the Workplace

A good day's work
*Bringing positive reiki energy
to your place of work may help
you to enjoy making a living
and give to the full.*

Y ou may like to offer reiki to a
colleague at work if he has had
a shock or is not feeling well.
Remember the reiki tradition: offer a
treatment only three times. If your offer is
not accepted, do not offer again. It is
probably particularly important to be
sensitive when offering reiki at work.

Reducing stress

There are various sources of stress
within the modern workplace, including
less than ideal working conditions, the
pressure of increasing workloads and

tight deadlines, the difficulties of
working with colleagues and managers,
and insufficient pay or time off.

Reiki may not bring about material
changes. However, it can change the
way in which you view difficulties, and
thus enable you to improve your coping
strategies. It is often helpful to send
distant reiki to your workplace, or to
your working relationships. You may like
to do this on your daily journey to work.

A short treatment

If a colleague accepts your offer of
reiki, ask him to sit comfortably, and
remove his shoes and spectacles, if he
is wearing them. Place one hand over
the third-eye chakra and the other on
the back of his head. Hold this position
for about three minutes.

If there is time, place your hands
over the temples, then over the ears, on
the back of the neck, and in front of the
throat chakra. Place one hand on the
upper chest and the other between the
shoulder blades. Move down to the
heart chakra, mirroring that hand on the

back, then treat the solar plexus, again
mirroring that hand on the back. Treat
the knees, hips, and lastly the feet. Hold
each position for two or three minutes.

Case History

Graham, 45, encountered a seemingly
insurmountable problem at work a few days
after his second-degree reiki course.

The main-parts warehouse at the company
where Graham works dispatched important
items to one of its satellite depots. To
Graham's dismay, the items did not arrive
and, despite frantic telephone calls, could not
be traced. The situation was made worse for
Graham because he was responsible for a
depot-stocking rationalization programme.
This had meant choosing a national operator
to support the company's requirements, and
this had been its first pick-up. Graham was
thrown into a panic but decided to send reiki
to the company. The next morning, Graham
received a telephone call to say that the items
had just arrived, although no-one could
explain where they had been. Graham gave
thanks to reiki healing.

Life Change

"I was surprised at the changes that reiki
brought to my life but I knew that it worked. It
had become a part of me." A reiki receiver

The sensitive touch
Once you have been attuned to reiki, your hands will tell you what you need to know.

HELPING OTHERS

Many people send distant reiki to their relatives and friends daily during difficult times at work or when they are sick. Reiki can be used to promote healing before and after an operation. Reiki is adaptable, so you can use distant-healing techniques, give a treatment, or simply hold the hand of the person you care about – whichever is appropriate.

Reach out with love
Reiki is of value not only to the patients in hospitals and hospices but also to the staff working there, to help them cope with the demands of their job. Reiki may also prove to be of comfort during bereavement and, for those who wish it, while dying.

Difficult moments
Knowing you are sending him reiki may help a friend through a work appraisal or meeting.

A light in the darkness
Reiki can help those who are seriously ill come to terms with their illness and situation.

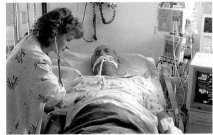

Reassure someone who is in pain that it is good to release emotions

Hands-on healing
Help to ground someone who is depressed by giving her reiki.

Use your hands to send reiki energy

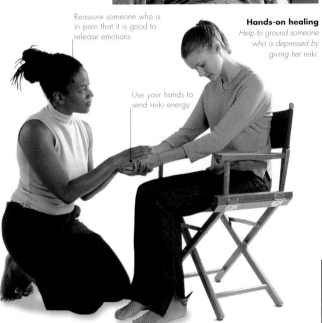

World Consciousness: the Way Forwards

Global harmony
Many of us long for peace and for a fairer world: reiki helps us to hold the vision.

Since the Second World War, the number of people practising reiki has grown rapidly. From its origins in Japan, it has spread to the West and all over the world, to people of different cultures, religions, and countries. Reiki practitioners believe that the growth of reiki has helped to raise the consciousness of many thousands of people, creating a network of positivity.

Reaching out

Reiki can offer strength, understanding, courage, and peace, not only to the individual and his circumstances, but to global situations. Some people send distant reiki to the Arab-Israeli conflict, to war-torn parts of the African continent, and to other parts of the world where anger, chaos, and disaster have undermined the harmonious way of living that all of us would choose.

Reiki Outreach International (see page 221 for contact details) is an organization that directs healing energy as often as possible towards world peace. You may wish to contact them with a view to contributing to a pooled effort of positivity.

Complete harmony

Some reiki practitioners share a vision that everyone in the world will come to know reiki and use it daily in their lives. They believe that the more people access reiki, the more peace and harmony will become part of the world's societies. This is not some utopian vision of total world peace being within easy reach. Rather, it works on the idea that as each person accesses his own inner calm and releases some of his negative behaviour traits, he becomes less likely to have a negative effect on those around him. Thus in a small way, each individual can add to the positivity of his own community.

Each teacher of reiki helps to increase the rate at which reiki spreads. The more people that practise reiki, the greater the benefit is thought to be. Some people liken reiki energy to a flame that is passed from person to person. The flame of one candle is not diminished as more candles are lit; instead there is more light.

Expanding Consciousness

If we sit still and expand the mind and the consciousness, its reflection, which is the visible world, expands and quietens also.

Bringing light
Reiki helps you in your personal development and encourages a lighter attitude towards life.

YOUR PERSONAL JOURNEY Different

people report different effects from having regular reiki treatments, and integrating reiki into their lives. These include a sense of personal freedom, a new ability to take control, and a confidence about following an individual path (see also pages 144–51). When you are attuned, you can choose to use reiki energy in different ways, to help yourself, to improve your personal circumstances, to help those close to you, and even as a vehicle to send your positive wishes for global peace. What you do with reiki is up to you.

Sending new signals
As they become more positive, some people find that they attract more positive, joyful people into their lives.

Flying into the unknown

Old habits and behaviour patterns can be hard to break, but reiki provides the starting point for life changes. Sometimes the first step can be easy: simply being able to see that there is more than one path to take in life.

Thought for the Day

Remember the reiki precepts, which are intended to help you develop a positive attitude. Repeating the following key phrases each morning and reminding yourself of them throughout the day can be a useful way to gain perspective.

- Just for today do not worry; just for today I am at peace.

- Just for today do not become angry; just for today my mind is at peace with itself.

- Honour your parents, elders, and teachers: I honour my parents, elders, teachers, children, friends, and myself.

- Earn your living honestly: I earn my living honestly and do no harm to anyone, anything, or the environment.

- Show gratitude to every living thing: I give thanks to every living thing and every situation, whatever form it may take, for their lessons in growth and understanding.

Daily practice

Greater positivity is one of reiki's greatest gifts. The precepts are there to remind you of this.

GLOSSARY

Attunement An initiation process that balances the chakras to alter the body's energy flow. This gives the person being attuned access to reiki energy and enables her to act as a conduit for healing.

Chakras The seven main centres of energy within the body. Each relates to different physical, emotional, and spiritual aspects of human life.

Distant healing A means of sending positive healing energy to people, places, situations, relationships, or objects.

Energy blockage When the flow of energy around the body becomes blocked, preventing the person from progressing.

Group healing Using more than one person to strengthen the effect of healing.

Healing crisis A temporary reaction in which the receiver feels much worse than before having a reiki.

Life-force energy Universal energy that is believed by reiki adherents to make up all things in the world.

Mantra Sacred name, given to each reiki symbol.

Reiki A hands-on form of healing that brings universal life-force energy to the recipient, helping to improve the flow of energy within her body.

Reiki master A person who has studied the first three or four levels of reiki and has been initiated by another reiki master.

Reiki precepts Five affirmations taught by the reiki founder Dr. Usui, to enhance daily living.

FURTHER READING

BAGINSKI, BODO J., and SHARAMON, SHALILA. *Reiki: Universal Life Energy* (Life Rhythmn, USA, 1988)

BARNETT, LIBBY, and CHAMBERS, MAGGIE, with DAVIDSON, SUSAN. *Reiki Energy Medicine* (Healing Arts Press, USA, 1996)

HABERLY, HELEN J. *Hawayo Takata's Story* (Archedigm Publications, USA, 1990)

HAY, LOUISE. *You Can Heal Your Life* (Hay House Inc., USA, 1999)

HORAN, PAULA. *Empowerment through Reiki* (Lotus Light Publications, Shangri-La Series, Germany and USA, 1989)

PARKES, CHRIS and PENNY. *Reiki: The Essential Guide to the Ancient Healing Art* (Vermilion, UK, 1998)

RAND, WILLIAM LEE. *Reiki: The Healing Touch* (Vision Publications, USA, 1991)

SHUFFREY, SANDI LEIR. *Teach Yourself Reiki* (Teach Yourself Books, UK, 2000)

SHUFFREY, SANDI LEIR. *Reiki: A Beginner's Guide* (Hodder & Stoughton, UK, 1999)

USEFUL ADDRESSES

Association of Reiki Professionals
P.O. Box 481, Winchester, MA 01890, USA
Tel: 781 729 3530

Guild of Complementary Practitioners
Liddell House, Liddell Close, Finchampstead,
Berks RG40 4NS, UK
Tel: 0118 9735757

Reiki Outreach International (Crisis Line)
USA: 916 863 1500

International Center for Reiki Training
21421 Hilltop St., No. 28
Southfield, MI 48034, USA
Tel: 248 948 8112

The Reiki Alliance International
PO Box 41, Cataldo,
ID 83810-1041, USA
Tel: 208 7833535

UK Reiki Federation
PO Box 261,
Wembley HAO 4FP, UK
www.reikifed.co.uk

Angela Robertshaw
20 High Street,
Albrighton, Wolverhampton
VV7 3JB, UK
Tel: 01902 374697
www.reiki-train.co.uk

INDEX

ACKNOWLEDGEMENTS

The publisher would like to express appreciation to Angela Robertshaw for reading and commenting on the manuscript of this book and for her help in the photography sessions. Special thanks go to the following for the kind loan of props or photographs: Naomi Blake; The New Academy Gallery, London; Cargo HomeShop, London; Phyllis Lei Furumoto; The Guide Dogs for the Blind Association; The Massage Table Store, London and Gloucestershire; and Debbie Moore for Pineapple.

Thanks also to Mark Ansari, Denise Christian, Michaela Clarke, Joy Duncan, Ben Evans, Klaus Heidensohn, Louis Heidensohn, Jamie Hickton, Pamela Hudson, Miranda La-Crette, Philip Ross, and Louise Sweeney for help with the photography.

PICTURE ACKNOWLEDGEMENTS

Every effort has been made to trace copyright holders and obtain permission. The publishers apologize for any omissions and would be pleased to make any necessary changes at subsequent printings.

A-Z Botanical Collection Anthony Cooper 27; **Houses & Interiors** Bruce Hemming 54b/Roger Brooks; **Phyllis Lei Furumoto** 29; **Powerstock Zefa** 23, 25, 39t, 39b/Randy Lincks 42/43t, 81, 82, 83b, 86tl, 146, 147b, 150/Kathleen Brown 151br/154, 155tl, 155bl, 155br, 169, 170, 171bl, 179tl, 193, 201, 203bl, 203tr, 203br, 204; **Science Photo Library**/Simon Fraser 14br/Dr Gopal Murti 15br/Royal Observatory, Edinburgh, 20/Keith Kent 22/Phil Jude 33br/Tony Craddock 34tl/John Eastcott & Yva Momatiuk 34br/Jim Selby 41/Simon Fraser 59/Sheila Terry 63bl/Mauro Fermariello 78bl/Brenda Tharp 86–87/Alfred Pasieka 145/G.Brad Lewis 149/Gary Retherford 151tl/David Nunuk 187bl/Jerry Mason 202/Scott Camazine 206tl/Crown copyright (Health & Safety Laboratory) 206br/Jerome Yeats 213/Blair Seitz 215; **The Guide Dogs for the Blind Association** 43b; **The New Academy Gallery** 95bl, 185